Engaging employees in changing times

The World of Stars and Rebels

Charles Barnascone

Published by Wisdom Publishing Ltd

Tel 01636 629002

Co-writer Christine Searancke

Editor: Ingrid St Clare

Editorial contributions: Laurice Barnascone, Tina Newton, Andy Hey

Design: Charlotte Mouncey

ISBN: 978-0-9558787-2-5

This book is dedicated to my wife Laurice a
daughter Serena both of whom have been a
source of love, inspiration, learning and s
for my ideas and ambitions.

Contents

Testimonials for *Engaging employees in changing times - The World of Stars & Rebels*

"As business leaders we have all been in Tom's position at one stage or other in our careers. What Charles does so well in this book is address these problems in a concise, easy to relate to structure. This book gives us the tools to deal with these situations and delivers a well-structured solution out of them."

Charles Nicholds – Managing Director – Murphy and Son Ltd

Through engaging, simple stories, Charles Barnascone demystifies what makes a successful business, what needs to be focused on for profitable growth, and for all elements of what is a dynamic, changing picture - to align. He discusses that engaged, enthused colleagues and delighted clients are the critical elements to focus on (not revenues or margins), but the latter is not possible without the former. This book details the necessary 'ingredients' and the 'recipe' to produce the holy grail of 'employee engagement'. And having been coached by Charles (the Magician for me) over many years at an individual and organisational level, I can testify that this approach is tried, tested and delivers results.

Michael Grace - Growth Director - SNC-Lavalin Atkins

"Charles writes with clarity and precision. Stars and Rebels cleverly blends story-telling with a direct narrative to provide business leaders with a toolkit of strategies to get the most from their people and achieve their business objectives. The author's breadth of commercial and academic knowledge comes together in a very readable format. We see a story told through the eyes of the lead character about decisions

and choices faced in their business matched with real-world commentary and exercises to allow the reader to apply the thought processes to their own business. The heart of the book focus' on enabling and empowering people to achieve their objectives. Charles reminds us that without good people in a business, there is no business. Too much focus on financial outcomes can cause directors and managers to lose sight of the aspirations and needs of the individuals until it is too late. Employee engagement is a key driver of success and by looking at the motivations and needs of their team, a leader can make changes to boost the detractors and stimulate the supporters. Stars and Rebels provides a roadmap for 21st-century business leaders to create the corporate environment to keep talented people on board and drive growth."

Paul Noble - Managing Director - Specialised Canvas Services Ltd

"The World of Stars & Rebels follows on from Charles's earlier book whose great insights into Leadership introduced us to the engaging parables of Tom and the Magician. This style of case study is particularly powerful when used with the intermediate exercises because the storyline and characters help maintain continuity and a context that a purely academic approach would lack.

The challenges of engaging people in your business are explored and explained here in detail and give support to the mantra that "Culture eats Strategy for breakfast"

Robert Day – Chairman and Founder – Blueprint Interiors

"Charles has a knack of simply explaining a complicated concept in such a way that afterwards you look back and wonder why you couldn't see the obvious. - The World of

Stars & Rebels does it again. "Why" you should be a good leader is obvious, "what" should be done less so. "How" can be a complete mystery. We all need to be reminded how to see the wood for the trees. Charles has managed again to explain a pragmatic path through a very complicated forest"

Shaun Coope – Operations Director – 2JCP Ltd

"How nice it is to take a brief respite from the day to day, to dip into your book and to remind myself of some of the key drivers that have got my business to where it is today - Not that I'm complacent, I can relate to Tom and I can definitely hear your voice in the words of The Magician! The beauty of the book is the clarity with which it illustrates what are fundamentally simple issues that are easily overlooked, but which are critical to the success of any dynamic business."
"I wish you well with the book, it has already reminded me of a couple of issues that I need to address - thank you 'Magician'!"

Jonathan Aldridge – Managing Director – Hydrogarden Ltd

"Having read the first book about Tom and The Magician I was delighted to receive the second. This book is everything a business leader needs to help them recognise the importance of understanding their business and the people in it. Reading it in story format allows the reader to relate to their own position and I personally found myself resonating situations and people in my own world. Understanding the importance of the rules of engagement and your team's values and work personalities has supported me in my leadership roles and then to further my career where I advise others of the same importance. Tom and The Magician's conversations

create penny dropping solutions that become clear why they are included, the further on you read.

Now I have this book I will be passing it on to my own clients to reinforce why I am encouraging implementation of the rules of engagement, and helping them with their work relationships from the rebels through to the stars. This book will be going straight into my toolbox and having it on hand to refer to. I'm looking forward to the third one already."

TJ Duncan Moir – Business Glu

"We as a business have been going through a transition of changing the team dynamics and future vision planning for the business after the impact of the past number of months. The story about Tom has been enlightening as I can really relate to the story and challenge. It has given me a number of points to think about, explore and implement over the coming months as we develop the new identity, strategy and systems for the future. I am a big believer that one can achieve a massive amount with the right team culture, supporting one another to grow, and driving the business success forward with common goals. Businesses don't stay the same and being aware of what change is occurring and what change to drive or expect is critical to keeping the balance and focus within the team. The questions the book has given me are what are the current dynamics, what tools can I introduce and what does the future team need to look like? Really inspiring read, giving a new form of thought towards team engagement and development."

Craig Harbron – Operations & Design Manager
– Bennett Engineering Design Solutions

"This is a great handbook for anyone running a business team no matter how small or large, all wrapped up in a lovely enjoyable story.

Business is always changing and so can the behaviours of your team so managing that is a key challenge for any successful business.

I really enjoyed this read, it's a very relevant story for any business leader, and I wish I had my own Magician!"

Chris |Jones – Managing Director – T3 Design Group

"There have been a lot of changes in Elta over the *years. Today we have the lowest headcount for over 10 years and yet we have grown sales and are more profitable. It has highlighted how having motivated people, focussed on specific activities, aligned with Business goals can create a great culture for them and the business to meet their goals.*

Just reading the first chapter encouraged me to draw and rethink department organisation charts and their structures, to identify my stars and rebels. It provided more clarity by just taking time to focus on what I had in front of me, plus discover where there were gaps to fill.

As a Manager my biggest challenge has been engaging employees so we all head in the same direction. You have been a constant aid to help me develop my leadership skills by applying the concepts used by Tom. I guess that makes you my magician.

I can relate my current and past experiences to those in this book. I have seen how just a few rebel employees can distract attention away from value add activities and prevent managers focussing on the employees keen to develop and achieve success whilst helping the business meet its goals.

I found Tom's story reminded me to take time to observe and re-evaluate my employees, as their needs and the needs of the business are constantly changing. The concepts in this book make the process a simpler one to apply and continue to revisit in the future as a refresher. Plus, re-reading Tom's story is easier than searching for a magician."

Damian Buxton – CEO - Elta Fans Applied Technology

Acknowledgements

I owe a huge debt of gratitude to the many people who have helped with this book. One of the absolute joys of training people, is that I'm constantly learning at the same time. I often say that I learn from my delegates as they learn from me. So if you have attended my workshops, you have probably contributed to this book in some way. Thank you.

Many people have provided kind comments, and words of encouragement about the book, some of whom were prepared to allow me to place their comments in print and by inclusion they have been acknowledged personally. Thank you to everyone who has provided ideas and contributions.

Thank you to the staff at Infinite Possibilities Ltd, both past and present, who have contributed to the success of our business, and created an environment where this book could be created.

A huge thank you to Laurice Barnascone, Tina Newton, Andy Hey and Ingrid St Clare, who worked patiently through the text, several times to make sure that I had communicated my messages clearly, and who provided invaluable feedback and support when it was necessary.

Thank you to Charlotte Mouncey, who brilliantly executed the design, and converted ideas, text and diagrams into something very readable, of which we can all be justifiably proud.

Finally, thank you to the late Christine Searancke, who started this book with me many years ago and unfortunately didn't get to see it finished. Thank you for the incredible contribution you have made to this book.

Getting the most from this book

How you read this book is up to you and will depend on your personal learning style and level of experience as a leader in engaging employees. The explanations of the concepts explored have been placed after each chapter to encourage you to complete the tasks while the story is fresh in your mind. If you prefer you may choose to complete the story before you begin the exercises.

The important thing is that you actually *do* the exercises.

This is what will make all the difference to your behaviours as a leader. Getting familiar with concepts intellectually is one thing, but it is nothing like as powerful as getting to grip with them practically. You need to apply them to your real-life situations when engaging your team.

When you do the tasks, give yourself the time and space to do them properly rather than rushing. Also, realise that if you are going to make a real difference to the engagement of your team, it will take time and they will need to be motivated. Set yourself realistic targets and celebrate small successes as you progress. This way you will integrate the changes into everything that you do and improve the way you lead others.

A word about pronouns. Throughout the book I have tried to balance gender. Within the story there is a mix of characters to reflect this. In the concepts section I have loosely alternated between my use of the male or female gender, simply because this is how the book flowed.

The concepts of leadership and employee engagement are not gender specific; it is simply easier to read than continually having his, her, or they, or him, her, or they, when giving explanation. Overall it is the concept being referred to that is more important than gender, and I hope this comes across as you read.

Finally, if you think that you recognise some of the characters, this is entirely coincidental. This is a fictional story with imaginary people, but they, and the situations in which they find themselves, are very much based on real life.

Introduction – Why Employee Engagement and Why Now?

Through a myriad of changing circumstances, employee engagement is one of the biggest leadership challenges we face today. If you have recruited recently you will know how frustrating the process of recruiting and engaging new staff can be, and that's only one aspect. People have information at their fingertips, whether they are choosing a product to buy or a career for the future, almost everything about your business is openly available, so a potential employee or customer can make an informed choice or form an opinion about your business.

A business can have clarity of purpose and very clear objectives, but if the employees have not bought into that purpose, and subsequently they have contact with your customers, there is a very significant risk that the customer will have an incongruent experience. This will potentially then generate negative feedback or comments, and a downward spiral.

If your employees are fully engaged, they will happily provide a congruent experience for your customer, and be proud to do so. That's what forms the basis of customer loyalty and repeat business, which is still the most cost effective form of business to win. If you plan to grow your business, the most profitable way is through repeat business and referrals. We all know this, and yet many managers are struggling to devote sufficient time to the development of the employees who will facilitate those repeat purchases.

This brings me to the second reason why employee engagement is critical to our time. Recruitment and retention of capable employees is a real challenge. The reason for this is that it is so easy for candidates to permanently have their CV online, waiting and watching for their next opportunity. If they were fully engaged in their job and their place of work and believed in the direction and purpose of the organisation, would they be doing this? Apparently not. A recent study by Ernst & Young highlighted that organisations with high levels of employee engagement find it twice as easy to recruit and four times easier to retain their employees than organisations with lower levels. For the first time ever, there are now more employees (77% in a recent study) choosing a job based more on the organisation's purpose and direction than on the financial package being offered.

When employees feel valued and engaged they perform better because they believe in what they are doing and the value they can add. If you combine the increased performance with the reduced recruitment and retention costs, employee engagement gives a phenomenal return on investment

All the current indicators and research are saying that the employees of the future will demand more clarity and expect great leadership. Those employers who provide this will outperform those who don't.

So, is it that simple, just provide great leadership to your employees and watch them and your business grow? Well, yes and no. Certainly leadership is a complex matter and there have been many leadership and management fads over the years. I've seen many come and go, some more effective than others, crucially there is one core theme which seems to hold true: if you build trust into your organisation so that people feel empowered to contribute to a well-known and understood destination or purpose, they will feel appreciated for a job well-done because they see progress, then you will get loyalty and great customer service in return.

Yes, I'm oversimplifying things; there is much more to it than that, and that's why you have a book in your hand not just a short article or a few paragraphs. There are still too many instances where the focus seems to be on cost and profit first, with what seems to be a management obsession with efficiency to drive cost out and treat employees like a resource to be used up. Yet, the reality is that customers soon tire of a cheap deal, and will be loyal to those organisations that they can see repay loyalty and care. That's where the long-term returns come from. When senior management heavyweights like Jack Welch – former CEO of General Electric, start saying that the only measures worth thinking about are employee engagement, customer satisfaction and cashflow, then it's time to pay attention.

This book will provide you with a perspective of how to engage your employees. It's written as a story, because stories help people understand and relate to a subject; that's why most wisdom throughout the ages is conveyed through stories. I hope that you enjoy the book and that you discover the lessons you wanted.

Chapter 1 – The warning

Tom stared at the CV on his desk; he could hardly believe his eyes. Three words reverberated round his head, "how could she?". They'd done so much together. In four short years they'd turned the business round from a handful of people struggling to stay solvent, to a thriving concern employing over 60 people and showing a very healthy bottom line.

Andrea was like his right hand. She was great with the staff, the customers loved her, and above all he relied on her to implement his ideas. She saw to the details and she followed things through. As if that wasn't enough, she managed the relationship with their biggest client; that contract had been the springboard for their change in fortune.

Over the years Tom had mentored and nurtured her, helping develop her innate talents into the excellent manager she was today. He knew she was under a bit of pressure, he'd seen that a few times recently. That's why he'd started looking for another manager to take on some of her work. But he hadn't expected the recruitment consultant to send him her CV!

Pushing back his chair with a sudden burst of energy, he thought about addressing it with her there and then. He stopped himself, suddenly aware that this wasn't the way to tackle things and he remembered she was on holiday anyway. In the old days he'd have phoned her mobile and asked exactly what she thought she was playing at, but over the years he'd learnt that probably wasn't the best way. Even he could see that the day before the Christmas break wasn't a good time to disturb her.

Just then Carla put her head round the door, smiled and said, "We're all going down to The Marlborough now, are you coming?"

"Of course I am," he replied dejectedly. "Someone's got to stay sober and keep an eye on Chris and Zeb. If they wind each other up like they did at the office party, they'll both be looking for a new job when we come back in January."

Picking up his coat he reflected that for the last few years he'd really enjoyed the traditional team drinks before the Christmas break. The whole team used to be there, but as the business had grown, fewer people seemed to bother. A bit like this year's party; only half the staff were there, and somehow it didn't have the same sparkle as before. People just didn't seem as excited as they used to be.

What a start to the festivities, he thought as the office door slammed behind him.

Late on Boxing Day night…

"For goodness sake, what's the matter?" snapped Tom's wife Suzie. They were sitting exhausted after a couple of days of presents and pantomime antics.

"Nothing," he replied.

"Don't give me that. You've been like a bear with a sore head all Christmas. You couldn't even smile at the pantomime." She paused to let him respond with the traditional, 'Oh yes I could!' but he just stared into the fire, so she went on, "I thought you said things were going really well." Still no reply. Finally she said, "Darling, we've been together 15 years, I know when something's wrong."

After a long pause, he said, "It's Andrea. She's leaving."

"What do you mean? I mean when? What will you do without her?"

Tom tried a half-hearted smile, then it all poured out, "To be honest, I just don't know. It's the worst Christmas present I can imagine. She does so much, holds everything together. To tell you the truth, I'd forgotten just how much she handles. This last couple of weeks with her on holiday has been a nightmare. I've had to deal with so much day-to-day trivia, not to mention all the office politics. It made me realise how much we need another manager, Andrea's said so for months. That's why I called the recruitment consultants I know and asked them to send me details of anyone they thought suitable. That's how Andrea's CV landed on my desk!"

Suzie put down her wine glass not knowing what to say next. They both stared into the fire in silence. Tom's mind was going round in the same negative whirl it had been in for the last three days. To Suzie it was all new. Slowly she started to realise what it might mean… Tom working late every night, bringing work home, snapping at the kids, having no time for her. She'd seen it all before, and she knew she needed to find a way to stop it happening again.

Suddenly she saw a glimmer of hope, "Have you thought about… well… you know… speaking to your friend, The Magician?" she asked quietly, "I know you haven't seen him for ages, but could that be part of the problem?"

Tom was about to dismiss the idea out of hand, but something she'd said struck a chord. Perhaps it was the wine or the warmth of the fire, but as he sat there he remembered how often The Magician had advised him to give himself time to think, and to listen to the quiet voice inside himself. Just then, the quiet voice seemed to be saying that Suzie's suggestion was a good one.

It was four years since he'd discovered the man he and Suzie called The Magician. Back then the business had been on the verge of going bust and things hadn't been great between him and Suzie either. The Magician had mysteriously appeared in his life and had gradually helped him to address all the issues. Tom called his friend The Magician because he seemed to appear 'like magic' and what he had suggested really worked. He realised it must've been three years since they'd last talked. Things had been going so well he hadn't felt like he'd needed him, and now they were so busy he didn't have time to think of such luxuries. Maybe that was part of the problem.

Tom wondered if The Magician could still be found. He only ever made himself available when Tom really needed him and he knew he needed him now. But he had to be relaxed, open and ready for any meeting. At the thought of talking with his friend and mentor Tom relaxed enough to put his arm around Suzie. Watching the dying flames flicker, he wondered where things had gone wrong.

The following afternoon…

Sitting on the bench near the sailing club, Tom looked at his watch again. He had waited nearly forty-five minutes. He was starting to get impatient. Suzie had taken the kids to her Mum's for the afternoon. It meant he could have some time on his own to connect up with The Magician. It had sounded a good plan that morning, but after sitting on the bench for so long he was starting to get cold. He was also beginning to have doubts, thinking maybe meeting with The Magician was not such a good idea anyway.

Eventually he decided he might as well go for a walk, *After all*, he said to himself, *I won't have much time for strolling by the sea once Andrea's gone!*

Half way along the headland he started to relax and enjoy himself. There was something about the sea that he always found calming. He watched the ebb and flow of the tide as a few gulls squawked in the winter sun. Just as he was about to turn back, he noticed a familiar figure standing a little further down the path. His heart thumped. Without even seeing the old man's face, Tom was certain it was the person he'd been looking for.

He almost broke into a run as he heard The Magician call to him, "Hello stranger, I've not seen you for a long while."

"What are you doing right down here?" Tom asked, with his grin of pleasure spreading from ear to ear. "I expected to find you where we first met. We often talked sitting on the bench by the clubhouse."

"Ah! Were you ready for me at the bench? Really

ready?" replied the older man with a twinkle in his eye.

Tom's instinctive reaction was to say "Yes!" but in his heart he knew it wasn't true. He knew from long experience that The Magician only made himself available when Tom was fully relaxed. Eventually he smiled wryly and admitted, "I suppose I wasn't."

"No, I didn't think you were either," said The Magician. He paused and continued "Well, it's good to see you, but I guess this isn't just a social call. Before you tell me what the problem is, why don't you fill me in on all that's been happening?"

It only took a few minutes for Tom to tell him how well things had been going and how they'd put in place lots of The Magician's suggestions. Finally, he got really excited as he explained that they'd a big new client coming on stream from February.

After a moment digesting all the news The Magician asked, "So is it a problem at home?"

"Oh no, Suzie and I are getting on fine, the twins are at school and Katie's top of her class in just about everything." Tom went on, "No, the problem's Andrea."

"Your number two?" said The Magician, thinking back. "She was a bit of a Star wasn't she? I remember she really responded to the time you spent with her. Didn't she run the business while you were in New Zealand?"

"That's right. I was so confident with the way she was running the business, in the end Suzie and I stayed out there for 6 weeks. Andrea had everything so well under control." Tom went on, "Then, last week I started looking for another manager, we're so busy we need another person. Anyway, the recruitment company sent me Andrea's CV."

The Magician was silent for a moment then said, "So your Star has turned into a bit of a Rebel, and a silent one at that - interesting."

"What?" asked Tom looking bemused, "What do you mean?... Stars?... Rebels?... it sounds like an American Football team!"

His companion laughed. "It's just a simple way to think about how people behave in a business. I'll explain while we walk back to the sailing club." They turned up the headland and The Magician went on, "Stars are the people who help you to drive the business forward. They tend to be bright and enthusiastic; the sort of people who lead the way. They are typically your key people, the ones you can rely on the most, but not necessarily at the top of your business, they could be anywhere. The key thing with a Star is that they are clearly pulling in the same direction as you. Rebels are like Stars in that they are very bright, but the opposite, in relation to direction. They generally do what they have to do to keep the boss happy, which can make them difficult to spot. They often seem to be pulling in a different direction from the rest of the team, almost like they are working to their own agenda and sometimes they're seen as cynical. With me so far?"

"I think so," replied Tom. "Only Andrea's always seemed like a Star to me, or at least she did. But what did you mean about her turning into a Rebel?"

"If someone who used to be a Star begins to feel

undervalued or frustrated or they disagree with the direction of the business, then they often disengage. That's when they have the potential to become a Rebel."

"But Andrea's never come across as cynical or disengaged. Well except when things are really hectic, like they are at the moment," said Tom.

"Good. That means she's probably only just started to be a Rebel. To begin with there's usually what I call a quiet rebellion, that's when they just disengage. It can be quite hard to notice especially if you aren't talking to the person regularly enough. The problem is that as they disengage, communication becomes less which makes things worse and the problem more difficult to spot." The Magician paused to see if Tom would react, but he didn't so he went on, "The second stage is called the noisy rebellion. This is where it can get more destructive as the Rebel starts to spread their negativity and cynicism throughout the business."

"This is all very well," interrupted Tom, getting frustrated. "Andrea's not cynical… but what am I going to do without my Star?"

"She hasn't told you she's going yet, has she?"

"Well no, but…"

The Magician pressed on, "Does anyone else know about her CV being in the market?"

"I don't think so, only me and Suzie."

"Good, so hopefully this is all just a well-timed wake-up call for you." He sighed and went on, "Look Tom, from what you've said I suspect the business is more than a little bit out of balance and that there are more people who are becoming disengaged. With luck, we can figure out what the problem is, get things back on track and still keep Andrea on board."

Tom looked sceptical, but all he said was, "So how do I do that and still get everything ready for a new client in February?"

"Well, you've got a few days between now and New Year, so start by thinking about all your staff and seeing how many Rebels you've actually got. I doubt if Andrea's the bad apple that started the rot. That's probably someone else. While you're doing that you can also identify the rest of your Stars."

The Magician put his hand in his pocket and passed Tom a piece of paper saying, "Have a think about these questions and let me know when you've got some answers."

What behaviours are you seeing that you don't want?

What behaviours are you seeing that you do want?

Who do you think are the Stars in your business?

Who do you think are the Rebels in your business?

Who's leading whom?

Tom looked at the questions, then said, "So will everyone be either a Star or a Rebel?"

"Oh no, you won't have many Stars or many Rebels, but I'm sure you've got a few. Most people are either what I call Willing Helpers or Fence Sitters, but we'll talk about those another day."

"But there are over 60 people now…" Tom's voice petered out as he realised he was talking to himself. The Magician always seemed to disappear once Tom was clear about what he needed to do next.

Gulls wheeled overhead. With a new spring in his step, Tom made for home. Yes, he wanted to get right down to thinking about the questions he'd been given. He was determined not to lose the easy, relaxed state that walking by the sea had opened within him.

Concept 1
Behaviours which indicate engagement – or a lack of engagement

Each chapter introduces you to a key concept. In Chapter 1 it is this: any organisation or team is a dynamic system. This dynamic system is alive and interacts with other individuals, teams and organisations in its own unique way. Any group of two or more people who work together for a common goal forms a dynamic system for the time that they work together. The behaviours which you see within the team are an indication of the levels of engagement of the people within that team.

The team or organisation responds to external stimuli in much the same way as a person does. However, the more people that work in a team or organisation the more complicated the system becomes. To maintain balance within the complexity, managers tend to put in place guidelines and protocols so that everyone knows what they are doing – the bigger the organisation, normally the more strict the rules.

The way in which team members interact with these rules will indicate their levels of engagement. If they fight against the rules either overtly or covertly, they could be considered as more disengaged, the more they align and support the rules and direction of the business, then they could be considered more engaged. The terms Star and

Rebel are used as an indicator of the level of positive or negative engagement.

You'll learn more about this later in the book, but for now just keep it in mind as you look at your own team or organisation.

In Chapter 1 you discovered that Tom has a business that employs over 60 people. On the surface things appear to be going very well, the business is growing, it is profitable and it is winning new customers. However, Tom has just discovered that his 'number two', the person he relies on most for the smooth running of the business, is looking for another job. Not only that, but he's discovered it through someone else, Andrea hasn't told him herself. This is one of many possible signs that all is not well in the whole organisation, not just in his relationship with Andrea.

Good managers need to be aware of the symptoms of engagement – they are powerful but sometimes very subtle indicators of what is really going on.

If we use the human body as an analogy, when a person is working too hard or not taking good care of themselves they might start to suffer from headaches or backache, or coughs and colds might linger longer than they should. If these symptoms are ignored and the person tries to carry on as usual, things keep getting worse until serious illness occurs and the person is forced to stop. The indicators of "dis-ease" are often subtle, and therefore sometimes missed. The human body will simply generate further symptoms until we pay attention.

It is the same in a team or business. In an organisational context there are many indicators that show the 'health' or 'fitness' of the organisation and it is important that these are looked at as a whole. Specific signs will depend on the team or organisation, however, broadly some examples are:

- Financial - profitability, turnover.
- Customer Service - levels of customer satisfaction, compliments, complaints.
- Staff - staff turnover, sickness rates, disciplinary and harassment issues.
- Sales and Marketing - market share, number of active customers, value per order, customer feedback, lifetime customer value.

For many businesses there is a tendency to over-focus on the financial indicators, but these can be misleading or very late indicators of employee engagement. Just like any team sport, if the competition is weak a poor team can still win, giving the impression that they are a good team, when in fact there are problems which were not drawn out by the competition – at least not yet. So even if a business has high sales and market share it can still be vulnerable to competitors who provide a better or more innovative service, or one that is more responsive to changes in customer needs. There are countless examples throughout history of organisations that were temporarily successful market leaders with no significant competition but were later beaten by a well organised competitor with highly engaged employees, seeing a market opportunity to be taken.

Probably the strongest and most important early indicator of the state of a team or organisation is the way the people in it behave. The reason this is a good indicator is that it is immediate. You can observe how a person approaches a task, how the team members communicate with each other, how they communicate with customers. The challenge is that behaviour can be difficult to measure or quantify. This doesn't make it any less a useful barometer to use to indicate the levels of employee engagement. As managers we need to be vigilant observers of behaviour and reactions.

Remember that for many organisations, a customer's abiding memory will be their last experience of interaction with an employee of that organisation, be it positive or negative. If the employees we interact with are properly engaged with the organisation's vision, our experience and therefore our memory of our experience will be in line with the vision.

This is why observing behaviours now is so critical to understanding the problems or successes, both present and future.

To help Tom consider the way people in his business are behaving, The Magician has asked him to think about who are the people behaving like Stars and who are the ones behaving like Rebels. As you will discover everyone has the potential to be either, but at any point in time there will usually be a few people in your team who are behaving like Stars and a few who are behaving like Rebels.

In simple terms a 'Star' is a person who is behaving in a way that supports you and your organisation's vision, objectives, values and identity. A 'Rebel' is someone who is less than supportive. A Rebel may even block progress although they probably wouldn't admit to it. People can and do change from one behaviour to the other very quickly depending on circumstances and the people who are leading them. For now, just consider the simple concept that people can be either Stars, Rebels or neither.

There are ways to gather data on levels of engagement, such as pre-structured online employee surveys to help you identify Stars and Rebels. Having access to tailored information like this will be very useful in verifying any problems in detail, so that you can identify what you have to do about them.

Your task:
Considering the people in your team or organisation, answer the four questions The Magician gave to Tom.

- What behaviours are you seeing that you don't want?
- What behaviours are you seeing that you do want?
- Who do you think are the Stars in your business?
- Who do you think are the Rebels in your business?
- Who is leading whom?

Summary:
In simple terms a Star is a person who is supportive of you and the organisation. They are pro-active and aligned with your direction.

A Rebel is a person who seems misaligned and disengaged with the business or organisation's direction. They are less than supportive and may even obstruct progress, although they may not admit it.

We will refine these definitions later; for now simply identify the people who fit into these categories. If there are any individuals you are not sure of then create a third list for these people.

The final question we should consider in this section is; who's leading whom?

The Magician asks this question of Tom to prompt some thinking about the probable cause of Tom's problems. Generating and keeping employee engagement is very much a leadership issue. At this stage we can probably surmise that Tom's leadership is under question, and that is very much implied by The Magician's comments, but this is a business of 60 people and Tom will not be the only leader.

Leadership should really be considered a mindset rather than a position, which means that leaders can come from almost anywhere in the organisation, from the most junior to the most senior, and the leaders in Tom's business will very much determine the culture of that business and therefore the behaviours which we see. We will be exploring this in much more detail later, but for now what the Magician is asking is who are the leaders in the business and who are the people being led. Is the leadership message which is being carried around the business in line with what Tom would like it to be and where is that message coming from?

The best indicators of that leadership message of course are the behaviours of the people within Tom's business. This is why we suggest that behaviours are such a good indicator.

The final question for you then in this section is asking you to identify who you think are the leaders in your team, business, or organisation? Who are they leading, and what is their message? Is the message consistent with the vision, mission, values of the business, and are the leaders consistent with each other?

Chapter 2 – Stars and Rebels

Tom sat in the cabin of the narrow boat looking at the two pieces of paper in front of him; one was a list of the people he employed, the other was almost blank. He'd drawn a line down the middle of the paper to make two columns; at the top of one column he'd written STAR, at the top of the other he'd written REBEL. Beneath the headings the page was empty.

He was struggling for inspiration.

Over the years he'd got into the habit of borrowing his parents' narrow boat when he wanted time to think. It was useful when he needed to get away from the distractions of the office and the family. Today it didn't seem to be helping Tom at all. Eventually he decided to make himself yet another cup of tea. Taking the steaming mug outside, he went to sit on the stern of the boat by the tiller so he could see the ducks swimming in the reeds. As he was watching, two of the smaller ducks seemed to be getting their feathers a bit ruffled. It reminded him of Chris and Zeb.

He'd liked both of them ever since they'd joined the company. Thinking back he realised it must have been over three years ago. Tom's business had needed trainees and Chris and Zeb had joined straight from college. They'd worked hard and been almost inseparable until Zeb had been promoted to team leader. At the time, Zeb had seemed to have a little bit more potential, but Tom remembered him and Andrea having long discussions about which of them it should be. Looking back that promotion didn't seem to have helped anyone.

Zeb wasn't performing well as a team leader. He was okay, but the team didn't really respect him. Chris on the other hand just seemed to have switched off and lost his motivation. He did what was asked of him, but there was none of his old enthusiasm. In fact, Tom realised that recently Chris had been going to the pub for a slightly extended lunch break with Rory and that was certainly something Tom didn't like.

Tom pulled his coat up round his ears as his mind turned to Rory. He often wondered what he'd done when he employed Rory, or Mr Grumpy as Carla called him. The only reason Tom had employed him was because he had all the specialist skills they'd desperately needed for a new contract. His skills and knowledge were second to none, and Tom was sure Rory was the best man in the country in his field. The problem was his attitude; he never smiled, he didn't like dealing with customers and he certainly couldn't be called a team player.

The only people Rory seemed to get on well with were the little group who went to the pub with him on a Friday. That little group was growing in size and starting to cause Tom to feel more than a little unsettled. It wasn't that Tom was a kill-joy. No, the problem was that Rory and his mates had a habit of extending their Friday lunch hour. They regularly didn't get back until 2.30pm when they should've been back at 2pm. Tom knew it was starting to upset other staff. He also knew he'd been trying to ignore the problem rather than risk a confrontation with Rory. The more he thought about it the more he saw Rory as a Rebel – with a capital R.

Once he'd realised Rory was what The Magician called a Rebel, Tom started to think about the other people who went to the pub with him. He considered Chris. The lad certainly wasn't as helpful as he had been, but he couldn't really be called a Rebel. However, the more he thought about it, the more he could see that Rory certainly wasn't a good influence on the younger man, or any of his other Friday lunchtime drinking buddies for that matter.

Realising this was just the sort of reflecting The Magician had intended, Tom decided to make a few notes while things were fresh in his mind. As he was finishing, his stomach's gurgling and grumbling reminded him of lunch. He realised he'd better return to the tiller and begin cruising upstream or he wouldn't get to his favourite pub in time.

Rounding a bend in the river he suddenly glimpsed a stag on the edge of the wood. It was standing perfectly still. Majestic. Imposing. Then it turned and bounded away. As he was reflecting on how impressive it was, he remembered he needed to think about the impressive people in his team as well as the Rebels. He said to himself "I've still got quite a bit of thinking to do if I'm going to identify my Stars as well as my Rebel. Still at least I've identified the real troublemaker!"

He noticed his favourite pub up ahead and decided to moor up nearby and enjoy a light lunch and a cold drink.

As he was mooring up and thinking about the delicious meal he was about to have, a voice beside him said, "So how's it going?"

Tom turned with a start, then realising it was The Magician said, "It always catches me out when you do that."

"Do what?"

"Appear suddenly. It's like you come out of thin air."

The Magician smiled, "I know this is your favourite pub along this stretch of the canal so I figured I'd join you for lunch. It's busy in there. Shall we just get a takeaway and eat on the boat?"

"I wasn't expecting to see you here, but it's good timing as I was just thinking about my Stars." He continued with a good deal of satisfaction in his voice "And, I've found the Rebel."

"Well that sounds like a good start. Go on then, tell me about them."

"All my top team are Stars," Tom said proudly, "Of course you know about Andrea, but you won't know about Terry; he's taken over the sales team; we employed him about 18 months ago. He's absolutely brilliant, a great sales person, everyone likes him. Well everyone except Suzie, but you can't please everyone all of the time can you?"

"Well no," replied his mentor with a note of concern in his voice, "But Suzie's always seemed a good judge of character. Why doesn't she like this chap?"

"She says the way he flirts with her makes her feel uncomfortable and she says he doesn't show me respect."

Tom went on, "I tell her she's imagining it; he's always fine when I'm around."

The Magician didn't talk any more about Terry, he just suggested Tom kept a note of Suzie's concern. He then said, "Who else is a Star?"

"Ingrid certainly is. We recruited her to look after finance a couple of years ago. She's got a system for everything, knows exactly what position we're in almost by the minute and she's brilliant at negotiations. I'd hate to play poker against her."

"She sounds ideal, what's her background?" The Magician asked.

"She did accountancy at university, then she went to work for one of the big firms, but she found it too impersonal and wanted more variety. We're really lucky to have got her. When our IT Manager left last year she took responsibility for all our IT and telecoms as well. She's saved us a fortune." Tom continued, "Now she's got everything well under control she's started studying for an MBA. It's a part-time course and it doesn't affect her work, but I think it will help the business...give us more of a strategic outlook, that sort of thing...anyway I've agreed we'll pay some of her costs."

The Magician reflected a moment, then asked Tom, "What happened to the girl who used to do your accounts? I seem to remember she was quite good."

"You're thinking of Carla," he replied. "She's a real treasure, always willing to help anyone. For example, a couple of months ago she helped one of our customers with a rush job. No one knew anything about it until the customer called Ingrid to query why they hadn't been charged anything extra. Carla hadn't even thought about charging them. She knew they needed the job doing urgently, so she got on and did it. Simple as that. I suppose you'd call her a Star, wouldn't you?"

"I'm not sure that I would," replied The Magician. "I think Carla might be more of a Willing Helper. That's one of the categories we haven't talked about yet. Willing Helpers are pretty much as the name suggests, always looking for ways to help. Similar to a Star, but they don't usually have as much self-confidence and they aren't as capable. As an example, you could say they help at a tactical level, but they don't see how to turn that help into an opportunity at a more strategic level."

"That's Carla exactly," Tom cried out. "She always underestimates herself. But when Andrea heard about that job, she came up with the idea of offering the same sort of fast turnaround to all our customers – but at a premium rate. It's proving to be quite a money spinner."

The Magician said, "That's a perfect example of the difference between a Willing Helper and a Star. The Star is more likely to spot the problem and identify a solution to it, and then implement the solution if it's within their job scope or authority. A Willing Helper will probably come to you with the idea, seeking reassurance to go ahead, and then expect a little guidance in implementing it, even if in reality they know how to implement the solution and they have the authority to do so. They need more of a coaching style you see. In a business your size you've probably got between five and ten Willing

Helpers. I'm sure you'll spot some more once you put your mind to it."

Tom nodded. His mind was already working on that.

"Before I go, I want to tell you about Fence Sitters. They're the fourth group. They're not Rebels, nor are they Willing Helpers and they certainly aren't Stars. However, they make up a significant part of most teams, and could be as high as 60% to 70% of a workforce in some teams. People who are Fence Sitters do what they have to, but they need leading and managing. As long as you have good leaders they'll follow and do what you need them to do, but if you have weak leaders your fence-sitters are more likely to follow the example set by Rebels."

Tom thought for a while about that, then he said, "So is it like a scale with Stars at the top, then Willing Helpers, then Fence Sitters and finally Rebels at the bottom."

"In some ways it is, but there's one real difference," replied The Magician, "Stars and Rebels share a lot of qualities with each other; they tend to be passionate about things they believe in, they're good communicators, they're internally motivated and they can lead others. It's the reason why Stars can become Rebels. Look, if you want to see it as an image it's like the line that you mentioned, but you pull the bottom of the line around so it's like a circle that doesn't quite close at the top. I've drawn it for you," said his mentor as he handed Tom a piece of paper.

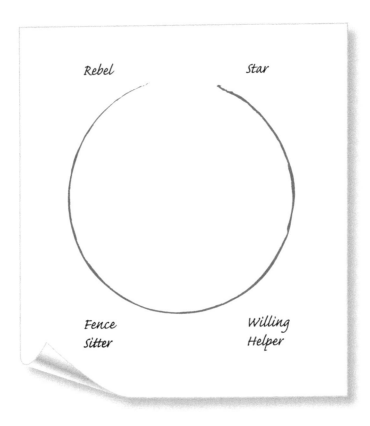

Tom looked at the diagram, "So do I need to think about the whole team in terms of who's a Star or a Rebel, a Willing Helper or a Fence Sitter?"

"Do you feel it would help you if you did?"

"Yes, yes it would," replied Tom.

"You might also consider how you're going to deal with each type differently."

"What do you mean by that?" asked Tom, but the older man had already disappeared, leaving another piece of paper with Tom.

> *Consider the members of your team who aren't Stars or Rebels:*
>
> *Who are Fence Sitters, who are Willing Helpers?*
>
> *How could you manage them differently?*

New Year's Day…

"Daddy, d'you have to go back to work tomorrow? We don't go back to school for almost another week."

The question came from Tom's daughter as they came home from walking the dog.

"I'm afraid I do sweetheart," he replied as he thought how quickly the Christmas break had gone by. His mind was already anticipating the conversation he would have with Andrea the following morning.

As he stood by the back door pulling off his walking boots, Suzie called to him, "Andrea's phoned, she's not going to be at work tomorrow. She's not well."

Tom groaned, this was all he needed. "What do you mean? Andrea's never ill."

"I spoke to her myself, she sounded awful. Apparently she's been at her brother's place for Christmas and she's been ill with the flu bug that's going around. Of course, her brother's a doctor and he thinks Andrea's run down and has been pushing herself far too hard. I must say I thought she looked a bit strained at the last office party. Anyway, her brother's insisting she stays with him until Thursday, then if she's feeling better she'll come home for the weekend and be in the office on Monday."

"Oh great," muttered Tom, "Another week coping without her, and another week not knowing whether she's serious about leaving!"

Concept 2
Behaviours – the tip of the iceberg, the gauge for future performance or problems.

In Chapter 2 you are shown different aspects of people's behaviour and you can begin to see how behaviours exhibited in a team or organisation can be seen as indicators of the health or fitness of that system.

The behaviours you see in the present moment are a good indicator of future performance, either positive or negative. Behaviours and results are the symptoms rather than the cause. In any team or organisation the results, whether financial, customer service or staff measures, are the product of the way the people consistently behave. Some of the behaviour is conscious and some of it will be unconscious.

Consider a sales team. It would appear that the better the team's behaviour, the better the results they will achieve. However, if they exhibit poor behaviour they can still get good results, but only in the short term. Either the results will dwindle from lack of activity, customers will tire of short-term tactics and gimmicks or a competitor will spot the opportunity and capitalise on it.

Behaviours differ from results in one key way – they are immediate. You can look at your team and see behaviours every moment of the day. However results often take a longer time to produce, especially in large organisations and those with complex products. It is the immediacy of behaviours that make them a crucial indicator for effective leaders and managers.

As highlighted before, to lead and manage a team effectively we need to keep aware of behaviours and any other information we can gain regarding the level of engagement of our employees. The level of engagement will affect every aspect of your business and eventually the results which you can measure, be they financial or otherwise.

In Chapter 2, The Magician explains a very simple, yet highly effective method of categorising behaviours. The four categories he creates are Stars, Rebels, Willing Helpers and Fence Sitters.

Remember these are *behaviour* types rather than *people* types, so a person could in theory at least, exhibit all the behaviour types in one day. Also the behaviour type can change given different circumstances or different leaders.

So you could have one leader thinking a team member is a Star while other leaders see them as a Rebel. Towards the end of the chapter this is starting to happen with Terry – Tom thinks he is a Star but Suzie has a very different view.

This situation illustrates how it is very beneficial to compare differences of opinion when thinking about your team. Behaviours can be easily misinterpreted. It's a bit like trying to read body language, when there are so many different potential meanings. This is where experienced managers will begin to trust their instincts about people. Arguably instincts come from simply having many experiences or reference points to call upon at the same time, which when combined together as a mass of information will be delivered as an instinct about something.

In the story, Suzie was calling upon her experiences of dealing with Terry and others like him and delivering what on the face of it is just an opinion, but good managers are well advised to pay attention to their own and others' instincts. Have you ever recruited somebody for a role when in hindsight they were the best of a relatively weak bunch of candidates? Your instincts were probably saying no, but to get the job done you ignored them and then it turned out to be a bad decision? We've all made such decisions. This is where having a second opinion works at its best. Tom needs to pay attention to Suzie his trusted ally.

Ideally we also need data. There are many ways to gather data about the level of engagement of employees, and my suggestion is that you do it regularly. As highlighted earlier, a person can switch from a supportive Star to a troublesome Rebel very quickly, and cause untold damage to the climate they are in. Having appropriate mechanisms to highlight problems and communicate with those involved are invaluable in keeping people engaged.

One of the reasons that Tom is so upset about potentially losing Andrea from his business, is that she has clearly in the past behaved very much as a Star. The business is dependent on her for part of its success, and Tom trusts her. She is a very useful ally to his business and he doesn't want to lose her.

This is one of the main attributes of Star behaviour - it gets things done and in turn engenders trust, but if the Star behaviour becomes rebellious and turns against you then you potentially have a formidable opponent.

That's why Tom is so upset. If Andrea turns against him, he's going to be in trouble and he knows it. So does Suzie, hence her comments when Tom first explained the problem over Christmas.

We will explore in more detail why Stars can switch to Rebels so quickly and apparently without warning, but as we described in the body analogy earlier, there are normally plenty of warnings of 'dis-ease' which are often ignored, either because we're busy, complacent or both. Then when they are noticed there is a lot of repair work to do.

Reviewing your team and their behaviours – a reminder

Before you think more about the behaviours you see in your team, here are some of the main indicators of the different types:

Star

Star behaviours are demonstrated by someone who is fully aligned with, actively demonstrates and 'lives' the team values. Their qualities may include:

- Good communicators, self-confident, quick thinking, optimistic.
- Well organised, multi-tasking, self-motivated and easy to delegate to.
- Proactive problem solving, spotting things that need fixing and fixing them.
- Often entrepreneurial, commercially astute, capitalising on opportunities.
- Potential to be good leaders.
- A Star is a useful ally and a formidable opponent.

Rebel

Rebel behaviour may express many qualities of Star behaviour, with the following differences:

- Misaligned with or disengaged from team values – or aligned to their personal agenda against the business. This may be because they feel 'ill-treated' by a leader currently or by one in the past. This would be their individual perception. Others in the organisation may or may not recognise or acknowledge their perceived 'ill-treatment'.

- Less situational confidence and more self-doubt than a Star and may take things personally, rather than having the awareness to let go of an issue and start afresh.
- They can be highly manipulative and they can be very clever in covering their tracks.
- Sometimes Rebels are 'used' to unsettle a situation or encouraged to cause 'trouble' and have then been treated as a scapegoat. This makes things very difficult for their next manager or leader, when trust between the Rebel and the 'management' has been damaged.

Rebel behaviour also has its own strengths and uses including:

- Highly effective change starters. They can challenge the status quo, are not always subtle, but often want to prove a point.
- Rebel behaviour needs clear and careful management and leadership. Left alone or ignored they will tend to become more disruptive.

Willing Helpers

Willing Helper behaviour is invaluable for getting the

majority of the usual tasks of the team completed as they are usually keen and willing to help you succeed. They often demonstrate loyalty and dedication to both their leader and the team. Watch out for the following potential challenges:

- Need clear leadership and coaching to support their development.
- They see their development as vital to their future and can quickly disengage to Fence Sitter if they are not supported.
- Optimistic – sometimes to the point of naivete.
- Trusting – they are likely to take something on face value which can catch them out later.
- Willing to learn new things but need help.
- Hesitant in taking action and look for affirmation when they have authority to do.
- Can solve problems, but don't always see the hidden opportunities.

Fence Sitter

When a person is behaving as a Fence Sitter they will work in the organisation to meet their personal needs at a very basic level – "it's a job, it pays the bills!" They are not inspired by their job unless they have a particularly inspiring leader. Watch out for the following behaviours:

- Below average willingness to learn new things
- Unreliable, seemingly disinterested in work and the organisation

- Can be easily led by either a Star or a Rebel.
- With a weak leader they will attempt to get away with doing very little and can be a drain on the team.
- Usually provides average performance, the plodder who gets things done if they have to but is hardly inspiring.
- Have varying levels of commitment to the team and the vision/values depending upon who they are interacting with at the time.

In any team the percentages of people exhibiting the behaviour types of Star, Rebel, Willing Helper and Fence Sitter will vary over time depending on the kind of organisation, the circumstances, the people within it and the way it is being led.

How to manage and engage the different styles and behaviours

You have probably already realised that these different styles of behaviour require different styles of management in order to get the best out of each. You've probably also spotted that while we're describing these as types of behaviour rather than types of people, that people do tend to have their default approach given a context or maybe a leader. So, a person could express natural Star tendencies for one leader and behave like an outright Rebel for another. We should ask, why is that? What generates such behaviour?

A person isn't permanently a Star, Rebel, Willing Helper or Fence Sitter, they can break out of these characteristics at any time, they are after all just behaviours. Human beings are also creatures of habit, and they gain some comfort from following their habits.

There is also an element of capability which we have to take into account. The Stars and Rebels tend to have more capability than the Willing Helpers and Fence Sitters. It could be argued whether this is intrinsic capability or applied capability – for example is the capability not there or is the Fence Sitter simply choosing to not apply their capability, or has their leader simply not been able to draw it out from the Fence Sitter?

The Magician showed the different styles as sitting on a circular line, rather than a straight one, if we add the element of capability – applied or otherwise – then this circle can be explained.

	Low alignment	High alignment
High Capability	Rebel	Star
Low capability	Fence Sitter	Willing Helper

As you can see from the model, the Willing Helper demonstrates a high level of alignment and typically therefore high engagement but a lower level of capability – often reflected in a lack of confidence, hence why they need support and re-assurance. The Star has a high level of capability and alignment, hence why they can just get on with things. The Rebel on the other hand typically has a high level of capability but is misaligned or disengaged. This awareness can then give us some clues regarding how the different styles can be managed and also what causes a Star to flip into a Rebel or indeed the opposite, a Rebel becoming a Star.

The clue is that this is often to do with trust and expectations. As you can see both the Star and the Rebel sit high on the capability scale. As the descriptions before show, they both demonstrate a good level of confidence, though if anything the Star would exhibit typically more confidence and openness for a given circumstance than the Rebel. So the question is what's the difference? Why is the Star aligned or engaged, and the Rebel misaligned or disengaged?

The answer is often down to vision and values. These might be historical or they might be current. In simple terms the Rebel either hasn't bought into, or is against the direction or values of the team at this time. This could happen for a whole host of reasons, but mostly it is because the Rebel does not see how the current circumstances, values or direction meet his personal values or expectations.

The more a Rebel trusts the leadership, the more likely the Rebel will align with the current or proposed direction. The less a Rebel trusts the leadership the more likely it is he will become increasingly rebellious against the current leadership or direction, at the same time often recruiting other members of the team to his way of thinking.

This makes a Rebel in a team dangerous for a couple of reasons; firstly, the lack of engagement of the individual is costly. A person with a high level of capability is probably paid well and is therefore relatively more expensive to employ. If you're not getting the best possible output from the individual, there's a lost opportunity. Also the problem gets worse. If you have a Rebel in your team, they can be quite influential with the rest of the team, particularly the Fence Sitters, so the lack of productivity can multiply out very quickly. You could have negative messages circulating around the team and affecting their engagement. This would explain the results of the series of recent Gallup surveys entitled 'the state of the global workforce' - which identified an average level of employee engagement worldwide being as low as 15%.

A point worthy of note here; alignment doesn't necessarily mean agreement. A Star will still argue with you if they see a potentially better way of achieving your goals. Notice that they are still heading in the same direction as you and are therefore not a Rebel. If they are prepared to argue a better way to achieve your goals, they are also probably expressing passion and motivation which needs harnessing and directing, not suppressing.

So, what do we need to do about this in the way we lead so that we engage the various behaviour styles and get the best from the team?

Let's assume that you have already communicated your vision for the team, their objectives, and have a mechanism for regularly communicating progress with those objectives. If you haven't communicated your vision or don't have one then logically that's where you start.

If you were managing a person exhibiting Star behaviour (high levels of capability and alignment/engagement) then the discussion should be focussed on WHY you want certain activities or objectives done, and how those activities connect to the vision and values of the team. The decisions regarding WHAT is to be done and HOW, would be made by the Star. You would take a very much facilitative style as the manager.

If you were managing a person exhibiting Willing Helper behaviour, you would take a much more coaching style. Just like the Star, explain the WHY. Then discuss WHAT needs doing and HOW, ask them open questions, have them discover that they do know how to do this with a few well-placed reminders, which will build the Willing Helper's confidence.

Next up, the Fence Sitters. Make the boundaries of the task crystal clear, including the WHY, the WHAT, and HOW. Outline the standards of performance you want and who they affect further down the line in terms of team members or customers. Make sure that they understand the consequences of getting this right and wrong, and that you are relying on them to get it right. Finally, check in periodically to see how they are getting on.

Finally, the tricky one, the Rebel. Now we have a dilemma. The common trap is to try to micromanage to try to control them. This would be the wrong move and cause them to rebel further. Remember that the Rebel has high levels of capability, so they can figure things out for themselves. The most important aspect to cover here is WHY you want them to do the task. The impact it has on the team, the customers, their colleagues. Get them to tell you how they would solve the problems of this task. If you disagree, tell them but you must explain WHY, and if you're going to suggest another way, explain why it is better for them and the business. Then, give them the responsibility for getting on with the task.

There should be no need to micromanage what they do, but you must discuss the results they achieved and how, after the completion of the task. Demonstrating that you trust them, might seem counter intuitive because you know they are misaligned, but remember they have the capability they just need to understand why they need to apply it. As long as you have agreed the WHY, the WHAT, the WHEN and the HOW in the prior discussion you can now hold them to account.

The thing to remember is that a Rebel hates being micromanaged. It implies a lack of trust, which causes more resentment when they already mistrust the management.

If you attempt to micromanage a person in Rebel mode, they will find a way to prove you wrong, and show that it's your fault that the tasks didn't get completed. You then will have difficulty managing the underperformance when you told them how to do it.

If you are seen to be fair and firm, then you can either; earn the respect of a Rebel by treating them fairly, and hopefully move them back into Star territory, or if that doesn't work out, have good reason to move them out of the team if necessary.

Chapter 3 – The revelation
- all is not what it seems!

The first day back…

Suja knocked on the door of Tom's office at exactly two-thirty. He'd expected her to be punctual, she'd always been reliable. They exchanged a few pleasantries about Christmas. She'd been with the company a long time, in fact she was one of the first people Tom had employed. Until Terry took over the sales team, Tom and Suja had spoken almost every day. He and Suzie had been guests at the wedding when she'd married Nic, and she'd had her little boy about the same time as Suzie had the twins. So they knew each other quite well, but even so Tom was wondering why she'd insisted on a meeting with him when Terry was her line manager now.

As soon as they were sitting down at Tom's desk, Suja blurted out, "I'm really sorry Tom, but I've come to resign."

At first Tom didn't know what to say. He'd thought of a few reasons for her wanting to see him, but this one hadn't crossed his mind.

After a moment he said, "But Suja, you've been with me almost from the start. What's brought this on? What are you going to do?"

"Nic and I have been talking a lot over Christmas. He's been promoted again, so we've decided we can afford for me to leave and then look for another job."

Tom's mind was quick to pick up on the fact that she

was leaving without somewhere to go. "What's upset you after all these years?" he asked.

She took a deep breath, then said, "That's why I insisted on seeing you. I don't like telling tales Tom, and I know you think Terry's brilliant, but," she searched for the right words and finally said, "He's just awful."

Tom could see Suja was struggling to keep her usual composure and whilst on the one hand he felt like dismissing what she'd said as rubbish, on the other hand he'd known Suja for a long time. He knew how loyal she'd been and he couldn't just brush this aside.

Gently he asked her what she meant, and then it was like the flood gates opening. Suja told him about Terry upsetting the girls with inappropriate comments and innuendos. Then she told him how Terry took the credit for sales which other members of the team secured. Finally, she told him Terry was developing his own business part-time. Everything else was taking second place, except of course, meetings where Tom was involved.

Once she'd poured out all the bad news they sat in silence whilst Suja got back some of her composure, "I know this will all be a surprise and you'll probably think I've made it up, but honestly Tom, I haven't exaggerated a thing. Everyone else is too scared to speak up in case Terry gets them sacked, but I don't care anymore. Nic says he's fed up with me getting stressed about it, so I'm going."

Tom glanced down at his desk. On it was the list of Stars and Rebels. Terry was at the top of the Stars but there was a little note by the side of his name. It said "Suzie – concerns".

He looked at the Willing Helper list and he realised that Suja's name was conspicuous by its absence. She'd been a great help to him in the past, but Terry had been saying that she wasn't doing very well. Tom hadn't thought that much about it, but now he began to wonder. Just who was telling him the truth?

He fetched them both another coffee, then he went into damage limitation mode. Eventually, Suja agreed that she would give Tom two weeks to do some discreet investigation into her allegations. It was clear that she didn't really want to go. Until Terry had arrived she'd loved her job. It was equally obvious that if Terry stayed, Suja would be leaving.

That evening Tom went home with a heavy heart. He usually talked to Suzie about things like this, but he already knew her opinion of Terry. No, there was no point Tom discussing this afternoon's bombshell with Suzie. And with Andrea at her brother's, he couldn't even phone her either.

The following morning Tom decided to have a closer look at the last few months' sales figures. The team were achieving their targets, so Tom hadn't needed to check the results in detail. After all, he thought to himself, that's why I employ Terry! A couple of hours later he realised he wasn't getting anywhere. The only thing he could really tell from the figures was that Andrea's operational team were getting a bigger percentage of the sales than they used to. But he knew that Andrea was always reminding her people that everyone who speaks to a customer has the potential to sell. For all he knew she was encouraging her team to get more sales without him even knowing.

Tom wanted to get someone else's opinion, someone who didn't work with Terry, someone impartial. Suddenly, Darren came into his mind. Darren was a senior manager with their biggest customer. It was he who'd given them a really great opportunity that had been the springboard for their growth three years ago. Andrea dealt with Darren and his team for operational things, but Tom had always managed the overall relationship. That had been until six months ago when Tom had handed the relationship over to Terry. Tom knew he would have to be discreet, but also felt he knew Darren well enough to get the information he needed.

Tom picked up the phone and dialled Darren's direct line, "Happy New Year Darren," he said cheerfully.

"Hello Tom, Happy New Year to you too," replied Darren instantly recognising the voice.

Tom went on, "I know you're always a busy man, but I just wanted to take the opportunity to check that everything's going okay with Terry. I hope he's looking after you."

There was a pause, "Well it's funny you should ask that, but I've been meaning to give you a call. To be honest I'm not that happy with him. In fact, I avoid speaking to him most of the time now. I deal with Andrea if I can."

Tom swallowed hard, then said, "I'm really sorry, I'd no idea you weren't happy or I'd have been in touch earlier."

"It's nothing major," Darren cut in, "It's just, you know,

his phone nearly always goes to voicemail and I never get as quick a response as I do with you and Andrea. As I say, just little things. Then before Christmas he upset our Purchasing Manager. I'm not sure what he said, she won't tell me, but I know she was livid. Anyway, I'd be happier if we went back to how things used to be, Tom, and deal direct with you or Andrea."

Later that day…

By the middle of the afternoon, Tom realised he couldn't sit at his desk a moment longer. He drove to the sailing club and walked along the headland. He wanted to see The Magician so badly, but he asked himself, how was he going to relax with all this in his mind? When he finally sat on the bench it was as though something snapped inside him and he gazed into the twilight.

"Well you look pretty miserable, what's happened? Have you found another Rebel?" said a familiar voice from behind.

"How did you know?"

"Just call it intuition," replied the older man. "Want to tell me about it?"

As The Magician sat down, Tom recounted the conversations with Suja and Darren and how the man Tom thought could do no wrong had suddenly become his worst nightmare.

The Magician listened to it all patiently then said, "Well Tom, it seems you've just learnt a valuable lesson about Rebels. As you've discovered, they often appear to be the brightest of Stars until you start to look rather more closely. Of course they're usually great communicators too, so most people fall for their plausible stories and ideas."

Tom asked, "Is Terry doing all this deliberately, I mean does he see himself as a Rebel?"

"Oh no. Terry will see his own behaviour from his own very different personal perspective. Our individual perspective is important, remember we perceive others in relation to our own values and beliefs. We'll see someone as a Star, a Rebel, A Willing Helper or a Fence Sitter according to our time, place and situation."

Tom thought for a minute, then said, "Ah! so that's why a Star can become a Rebel if they stop feeling valued or supported."

"Exactly. And remember, it's a scale. A person might be close to being a Star today but more of a Willing Helper tomorrow. A Fence Sitter may be drawn towards being a Willing Helper by a manager who's a Star, but they could easily become more rebellious if they're led by a Rebel."

Finally, The Magician said, "What's happening with your real Star? What about Andrea?"

"Happening," replied Tom, "Nothing's happening. She's off sick. At least, I hope that's where she is…"

"I find it interesting that you have found another Rebel. There's a pattern forming here Tom. Bearing in mind what you've discovered about Terry, you might like to think again about your original list." "Here are some questions which might help." The Magician handed Tom a rolled up piece of paper. As he read it and reflected on the questions being asked he looked out to sea, enjoying the view he'd seen so many times, thoughts drifting in and out of his mind.

When his attention was drawn back to the seat, The Magician was gone.

Review the list of Stars, Rebels, Fence Sitters and Willing Helpers.

Does this label apply to this person all the time?

Under what circumstances are they different?

What are you doing differently as their leader to encourage or suppress their behaviour?

What else could be encouraging the behaviour you're seeing?

Concept 3
Team identity/culture model

One of the most common questions I get is how do these behaviours come about, what causes a person to move from Star behaviour to Rebel behaviour and can we get them to change back. The answer is that there are many causes which we will explore and that depending on how much the Rebel identifies with being a Rebel, it is possible to pull them back. Hence the comment from The Magician right at the begining of the story "With luck, we can figure out what the problem is, get things back on track, and still keep Andrea on board."

We now need to look at the causes of the behaviours we have identified. To do this let's explore a simple model, which can begin to highlight the causes of the four types of behaviour identified. The model is on the next page.

The behaviours we have described sit in the outer ring of this model; they are an 'effect' of one or more of the causal inner rings. In other words the behaviours we see in team members may have several causes which will typically sit within the inner rings.

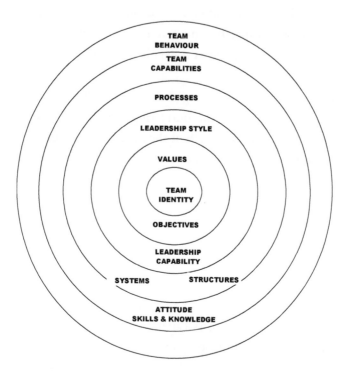

To illustrate the point here let's look at some examples:

- Team and individual behaviour might be driven by a reward or bonus system for specific activity or results – which would be a process driven behaviour.
- Team leaders might instruct team members to behave in a certain way – which would be a leadership driven behaviour.

- Objectives could be set and agreed to complete a task in a specific time frame – which would be an objectives or values driven behaviour.

To diagnose a cause using this diagram, the principle is that we start with the outer rings and steadily work inwards, identifying which of the inner rings are causing or contributing to the outer ring behaviour.

The further into the rings we go, usually the more effect the rings have, so for example, leadership style or methods, would probably have a deeper causal relationship in the long run than capability or training.

So let's start with the outer rings. Firstly, behaviours are the result of the person's capabilities – what they have learned to do or not do. Capabilities are not just their natural aptitude but also what they have been taught to do or not do in the past. People tend to be creatures of habit. In his book The 7 Habits of Highly Effective People, Stephen Covey referred to habits being made of three things; knowledge, skills and attitude. If all three are aligned then a person has the knowledge of what to do, the skills of how to do it and the attitude of wanting to do it.

In order for an action to become a behaviour, the same principle applies: behaviours need to repeat so we treat them as having the same ingredients as a habit.

With knowledge, skill, attitude and repetition in place the capability is more likely to become a habit. A behaviour then could be something that a person has learned to do and likes doing. The cause probably being training, coaching and practice. If a person is <u>trained</u> to behave in a particular way we should expect that behaviour.

So let's move in to the next layer of the diagram. Another causal factor would be the systems, structures or processes people work within. Through these systems and structures the team are encouraged or rewarded for what they do or do not do. In a business sense a system might be a standard operating procedure to follow, or a reward system which highlights and encourages a particular set of behaviours. Systems can also work negatively, penalising a behaviour, therefore encouraging a person to stop that behaviour. If you <u>reward</u> a person to behave in a particular way we should expect that behaviour.

Next layer – leadership. Behaviours are also affected by what team members are told or shown to do or not do by the leaders of the team. The team behaviour is therefore a consequence of what the leader does or doesn't do. It is possible that a behaviour could be encouraged by the *lack* of a leadership message, or the *lack* of a system or process. So in the absence of proper leadership you might get the wrong behaviours because the right behaviours aren't being encouraged. If you <u>lead</u> a person to behave in a particular way we should expect that behaviour.

Finally, the intrinsic values – what the team 'rules' say they should do or not do – affects an individual's behaviour. This is of course providing that the values of the business have been communicated. Like the leadership layer above, in the absence of team or organisation values people will assume their own apply and this can cause friction in the team when people aren't clear what's important. In effect, the outer rings of behaviour and capability are the 'product' of the inner rings of systems, structures, processes, leadership and team values.

Objectives and values sit at the same logical level in the diagram because when we set objectives we are declaring them as important within the business, as having value. If you set a profit objective for example you are declaring profit as important, like a value. Equally we might set a customer service standard objective, thus declaring customer service as important and having value.

Let's look at some examples of what could happen in different situations.

A person could exhibit Fence Sitter behaviour because they are not being led clearly (absence of leadership) or measured properly (absence of systems), so they can 'get away with' poor performance.

A Star becomes a Rebel over time because the leader makes promises, which he can't or won't keep. This indicates a lack of leadership integrity. The Star becomes frustrated that his needs or expectations (often individual values) aren't being met and so becomes more and more negative towards the organisation or the leader.

A Willing Helper is coached and supported (positive leadership) by her leader to become a Star. The leader delegates more responsibilities and provides opportunities for the development of her commercial awareness (capability), clearly defining her role and agreeing expectations (objectives and values).

A Rebel is 'converted' into a Star by a leader who is prepared to start afresh, gain understanding of the Rebel's values and what drives and motivates his behaviour. A good leader adapts his leadership style (positive leadership) to connect with the Rebel and convert him to a Star.

The main point to remember here is that the behaviour we see is 'caused' by the presence or absence of an element shown within the inner circles. People adapt their behaviours based on the elements within the inner circles in order to achieve success. The outer behaviour is a 'product' of the inner circles.

As an example of what could happen, if a leader does not tackle poor discipline or organisation within a team, the absence of leadership in this area 'teaches' the team members that poor discipline or lack of organisation is OK and that becomes the norm within the team.

What happens if a reward system encourages behaviour which is misaligned with the team objectives? A bonus scheme which rewards customer service agents achieving higher call volumes, for example, could be to the detriment of good service by encouraging an agent to end calls quickly to hit high call volume targets and bonuses rather than solve the client problem properly.

In the story Tom considers Terry to be a star. Terry appears to be getting results but as Tom later sees, he is doing so at the expense of team engagement. The question we need to ask is what is causing or allowed this to happen? To identify this we look at the inner circles and it will be one or more of these 'levels', which identify the answer.

Again let's look at these circles from the outside in.

Capability – was Terry 'trained' to behave this way? This may be a pattern he learned early in life to achieve his own selfish ends. Tom may have inadvertently created circumstances that allowed him to continue this behaviour. Certainly the impression that we are given is that Tom trusted Terry and left him to get on with the task of leading the sales team. What transpires is that Terry had achieved his success on the back of others without giving appropriate credit, and had benefitted from the already positive reputation the company had with its customers. Terry appeared not to be bringing new business, but there was very little oversight or leadership from Tom, and it's not clear if this was set as an objective.

Processes – Was there a system which encouraged this behaviour or the absence of a system to prevent it? Probably an absence of a system of communication, as we will see later!

Leadership – Did Tom as the leader allow this to happen and so encourage Terry to abuse Tom's trust? Almost certainly Tom's leadership or lack of it led to this situation. If anything Tom is guilty of giving too much trust and not checking on progress with Terry in sufficient detail to begin to see the problems forming. The best way to evaluate a leader is to get feedback from the people being led. Tom clearly didn't do this with Terry's team, otherwise he would have seen the warning signs much earlier. There are formal ways to do this which are very easily implemented, such as using 360 degree feedback reports or carrying out regular feedback reviews of the whole team to understand their perspective and address their concerns.

Your task:
Write a list of all the people in your team. Make a note alongside their name of the behaviour type (Star, Willing Helper, Fence Sitter, Rebel) they seem to spend *most* of their time displaying.

Consider whether this changes given different circumstances, different leaders or different colleagues they work with.

What is driving this behaviour? Past circumstances or current circumstances? Consider the inner circles of the team identity model, which of these inner circles are the cause of, or have contributed to, the behaviour as you see it. Remember it could be the presence or absence of a key element from the inner circles.

We will explore later what you need to do as a good leader to either sustain this behaviour or correct it.

Chapter 4 – The re-evaluation

Monday morning…

Andrea and Tom both arrived at the office early. They'd spoken briefly by phone the day before and agreed that they would need at least a couple of hours to catch up.

After his discussion with The Magician, Tom had thought hard about how to approach the meeting. He really wanted Andrea to stay, but he also recognised that if it was time for her to move on it was better done amicably than by turning his Star into a Rebel.

He closed the office door and asked how she was feeling. She'd said on the phone that she was a lot better, but he could see she still wasn't back to her usual energetic self.

Typically Andrea dismissed his concerns and asked, "So what's happened while I've been away?"

Tom knew she was meaning in terms of customers and staff, but it was the opening he'd been hoping for. "To be honest, I've had a few surprises," he said, then went on, "The first one was when I realised just how much work you handle in a day. Your team were brilliant at dealing with the day-to-day operational stuff, but all the HR and training queries and anything out of the ordinary all came to me. It made me see how desperately we need another manager to handle all that."

"I've been telling you that for 12 months," Andrea interjected, half exasperated it had taken so long for Tom to realise and half relieved that he might finally take some action.

"I know, I know" admitted Tom, putting a hand up apologetically to stop her saying anymore. "But that just gave me a bigger surprise. You see I called a person at a local recruitment company I met at a recent networking event we went to. This is what they sent me." He pushed the pile of CVs across the desk towards Andrea. Hers was on the top.

If she'd looked pale when she walked in, her face was now bright crimson. "But I only sent it to them just before Christmas. I mean, they weren't supposed to submit it to anyone without asking me, and …" Her voice tailed off. For once Andrea was lost for words.

"Look I'll be honest with you," said Tom seizing the initiative, "I don't want to lose you, but if it's time for you to move on I'd rather you'd told me than let me find out like this."

"I've been thinking about what to do all over Christmas. My brother's sick of me talking about whether I should stay or go. The only reason I sent my CV out to that agency was because I was so annoyed when you insisted on sticking to the holiday policy and made me take those two weeks off before Christmas."

Tom sat quietly as Andrea went on, "I'd nothing planned, so I was sitting around at home worrying about the huge amount of work I'd have to do when I got back. Then once I'd slowed down I realised how tired I was. I'd worked flat out for six months. I'd told you so often we needed an HR Manager, I was starting to think it would never happen. Then I forgot to divert my mobile one day and Darren phoned wanting something because Terry hadn't called him back. That was the last straw."

"So you decided to see what other jobs were out there?" suggested Tom, as Andrea seemed to run out of things to say.

"That's about it," she replied.

"But you and Terry get on quite well don't you?" asked Tom.

"I suppose so."

"You don't sound very convincing" said Tom, "Please Andrea tell me what you really think?"

Andrea sighed, "For what it's worth, I think the man's a complete waste of space, but I know you think he's wonderful and you're the boss."

"What do you mean 'you're the boss'?" asked Tom. "Surely we're a team, I've always valued your opinion."

"I think you used to value my opinion," Andrea agreed. "But now you only talk to me when we've got a serious problem. The rest of the time you seem to be talking to either Terry or Ingrid. Operations is always less glamorous than Sales and Finance. We're just the ones who actually do the work."

Tom had never heard Andrea talk like this. She sounded quite bitter.

"Andrea, you know I think you're an absolute Star," but even as he was saying it, Tom knew Andrea didn't know that anymore, and he knew he didn't treat her that way. He'd been taking her for granted and not giving her praise when it was due. He could see that all too clearly now. "I may not have said it for a long time, but this business needs you and just about everyone here thinks you're a Star. It's not just the team, our customers think you're great too, especially Darren."

That made Andrea smile, she and Darren had always got on well. "Why have you been talking to him?" she asked. "Is that another problem?"

"Just a bit," replied Tom sighing. He went on to tell her briefly about his conversations with Suja and Darren. Finally he said, "I think you and I need to spend more time talking to each other, like we used to. Let's check our diaries and find the first half-day we're both free. We'll get out of the office and find somewhere we can talk all this through."

Friday morning…

"So have we covered all the operational issues that are concerning you?" asked Tom.

"Yes," Andrea replied, satisfied that they had agreed actions, timescales and responsibilities to resolve a number of things on her list.

"And you're really not going to pursue looking for another job?"

"No, not now we're getting things sorted."

"Great," replied Tom noticing that she had a touch of her usual sparkle back. He looked at his watch. It was just eleven o'clock and they weren't expected in the office until the afternoon, so they had plenty of time to discuss one more thing before sharing an unhurried lunch.

"Go on then, tell me what 'Stars and Rebels' means," said Andrea. It was the last item on the agenda.

Tom explained to her about Stars, Rebels, Willing Helpers and Fence Sitters. Then asked if she would go through all the staff with him, linking each person to the scale based on the person's behaviour. Two things soon became apparent; firstly that Andrea had much more contact with most of the staff than Tom, and secondly how different their perceptions were for some people, but how similar they were for the majority.

Something they agreed on was the identity of their number one Rebel. It was Terry. Their first discussion of the morning had been about him. During the previous few days they had both been making discreet investigations and uncovered quite a lot they didn't like. It was clear that one way or another Terry would soon be leaving the business. Their concern now was less about him and more about the way he might be a negative influence on others, but they were already realising that Terry was so busy building his own business that he didn't have much time to influence anyone else.

They turned their attention to Rory. Andrea said, "I know we employed him because of his specialist skills and knowledge, but on that HR course you sent me on, they were adamant that you should always consider attitude first."

"Yes, I know," agreed Tom, "I've had misgivings since his first week, but we've still got the question of could we cope without him?"

"We do when he's on holiday," replied Andrea, "and when he's ill. We coped for a month last summer when he had that operation on his foot. I know Rory says Chris is useless, but the customers didn't complain when Chris went out to them in place of Rory."

"You say that, but Chris has joined Rory's Friday lunchtime drinking buddies."

"Yes, I'd noticed," admitted Andrea. "But we used to think Chris had lots of potential. Do you think we mismanaged him, maybe he lost his confidence when we promoted Zeb?"

"That's just what I've been wondering," said Tom. "I certainly think we need to manage Rory more firmly, and you're right, if we can cope without him for a month, we may be able to cope without him completely. Maybe without his influence we can turn Chris around too. Chris might be a Fence Sitter who's responding to a negative influence."

Andrea interjected, "Let's not write off Rory just yet either. I think he's had things too much his own way. I understand what my other teams do, but Rory's stuff is so specialist I've never really got to grips with it. So I leave him pretty much to himself." She paused for a moment reflecting, "I should have taken a tougher line with him from the start too, but I think we were both always afraid we would struggle technically without him. I'll have a word with him."

"Great," said Tom pleased that Andrea was very much back to her old self, taking responsibility for everything operational.

"Tom, I think there's something else we need to consider at the same time as the Stars and Rebels attitudes and behaviour stuff."

"What's that?"

"Developing capability," she paused. "We've never really thought about whether our people are using their knowledge and skills as well as they could be. I learnt about it on that HR course, but I've never had time to put it into practice. I've probably got the notes somewhere; hopefully I can still make sense of them. Of course when we employ our HR Manager they should know, but I don't feel we should wait that long."

"No, nor do I," replied Tom. "But I think I know someone else who might be able to help us. Come on, we've done enough thinking for one day. Let's go and get some lunch. Then this afternoon I'll have a chat with Terry."

Andrea smiled at him as she gathered her papers together and said decisively, "And I'll remind Rory just what time his lunch hour ends."

Saturday morning…

Tom drew back the curtains to reveal the dark winter morning; it was cold and crisp, the ground covered with a light frost. Saturday mornings meant two things for Tom; firstly walking the dog with his little girl, Katie, and secondly, his weekly game of golf with his old friend PJ. He always looked forward to both and this morning was no exception.

It had been a long and trying week, but Tom knew that an hour hearing about Katie's exploits at school would soon put everything into perspective.

That morning they had a particularly lovely walk as

Katie was entranced by the pretty patterns of the frost. The previous day's difficult interview with Terry seemed a world away. The meeting had been acrimonious at times, ending with Terry resigning and Tom asking him to clear his desk and leave the building. Now as Tom threw another stick for Barney and looked at the clear blue sky, he felt confident that things were really starting to move forward.

An hour later, he was loading the car with his golf clubs as the phone rang. It was PJ, "Tom, I'm really sorry mate, but Sandra's got this dreaded flu bug, so I'm going to have to stay at home and look after the kids."

"But PJ, I was going to beat you!" exclaimed Tom.

"Well that rare and momentous occasion will have to wait for another day," laughed PJ as he put the phone down.

Sighing, Tom started to remove his clubs back out of the car, but then he told himself he deserved his bit of rest and relaxation. Besides he needed the practice if he really was going to beat PJ next week.

As he was walking off the 18th green towards the club house, feeling quite content with the world, a voice by his side said, "I'm glad to see you're still making a bit of time for yourself. Everyone needs some time to reflect."

"I certainly need it after last week," was Tom's quick-fire reply as he turned to smile at The Magician. Barely pausing to take in his friend's mysterious appearance he continued, "I suppose you want to know what happened."

"You could say I'm a little curious."

Tom hardly waited for the response before he went on, "The best news is that Andrea is definitely staying. And, we're going to work more closely together like we used to. We've already had a couple of very productive meetings and you'll be pleased to hear we've been thinking about our Stars and Rebels. There's something I want to ask you about, but I'll tell you the other news first."

"Okay," replied The Magician listening attentively.

"It all happened yesterday afternoon. I spoke to Terry and Andrea spoke to Rory." He paused, before continuing. "My meeting with Terry was awful, I saw a totally different side to him, he was like another person. I spent what felt like hours going over it with Suzie last night, as usual she listened and was really supportive despite the fact that I ignored her early concerns about Terry, but the main thing is he's resigned and gone and all I can say is good riddance. I don't think it'll do us any long-term damage, but it does mean I'll have to head up the sales team until we find a replacement. I've an idea the sales pipeline is almost non-existent, but I'm going into the office tomorrow to get an idea of how bad things are before the weekly sales meeting on Monday."

"I'm sure you'll soon have that well under control," said his mentor, "But how did Andrea get on with Rory?"

"Well that was a bit of a revelation too; but a positive one. Andrea thinks Rory has more potential than we ever realised."

"Really?" said The Magician with a twinkle in his eye.

"Yes, she says there's a side to him we never see. Apparently he has a little girl. Rory and her mother split up years ago; she moved to the city and took their daughter with her, but every Saturday Rory drives over and takes the girl out for the day. Andrea says he's like a different person when he talks about her."

"That's good to know," said The Magician, "but how does it help you and the business?"

"Andrea found out, because she was doing what you told me to do years ago."

"Really. And what's that?"

"Ask people what's important to them," replied Tom. "As soon as Andrea started to take an interest in something that mattered to Rory, he started to open up and talk to her. Andrea's convinced now that she's mismanaged him. In fairness I think we both have, his work's so specialised we just leave him to get on with it, especially as he's usually so difficult to talk to and everything looked like it was going OK. Anyway Andrea's asked him to spend some time thinking about what's important to him in terms of his work, and they're going to talk again next week."

"What about his extended lunch hours?" asked The Magician.

"Apparently he'd never really thought about it. He works late most days, which is true and doesn't claim any overtime, so he thought there was no harm extending his lunch hour a bit in return. When Andrea pointed out that it wasn't a very good example for the rest of the team, especially the youngsters, he was amazed at the idea that anyone took any notice of what he did."

"So you think he'll change his habits now, do you?"

Tom replied, "I think he might. You see, Andrea asked if he'd help her by thinking of himself more as a role model for others, just like he is for his daughter. She says he responded really positively to that."

The Magician nodded and said, "So you're hoping that one of your Rebels might be turned into a Willing Helper or even a Star, are you?"

"It'll probably take a long time, but maybe a Willing Helper." Tom went on, "On the technical side he's second to none. Customers are always pleased with the work he does. Now, that reminds me, I wanted to ask you about Skills and Knowledge."

"Ah," replied The Magician, "I wondered when you'd realise that attitude and behaviour are only a part of the picture."

"Before we move on to skills and knowledge Tom, I think it would help to think about what's important to your people and how it relates to their behaviour. These questions might help." The Magician passed Tom a note of the questions.

Tom read them through.

Identify the behaviours you would like to see from the team day-to-day.

To get those behaviours consistently, what attitudes would need to be present within the team, and what would have to be important to them?

Consider those who may be Fence Sitters or Rebels. What different behaviours you would like to see them express, for you to feel like they are more engaged?

What behaviours would you like to see them stop doing?

Consider those who are Stars and Willing Helpers. What behaviours are you getting that you want, and what do you need to do to keep them engaged?

"So Tom, do you have some way of identifying the capabilities a person needs to be successful at their job and a way of developing those capabilities? It might be a job description or a competency profile for each of the positions in the business?"

"We have job descriptions, but to be honest they're a bit vague and we haven't updated them recently. We did them after you suggested we review our business systems, but that was over three years ago."

"When you get your new HR and Training Manager, one of their main tasks should be to ensure that the company identifies the skills and knowledge needed for each role and continually reviews how well each member of staff matches the ideal for their role. Any gaps between the competency profile and the actual ability will show where people need some type of training or development. They can also have a development discussion around career goals and aligning to the goals of the company. This will be the first step in making sure that you regularly develop your people. As your business grows you'll have more demand for capable people with strong skills and knowledge and the probability is that you'll need to develop them yourselves rather than buy capability in. It's typically better to recruit a person with the right attitude and develop them internally."

Tom registered that The Magician had just said something Andrea had mentioned only a few days ago when talking about Rory – recruit for attitude first, you can develop knowledge and skill.

"Fair point about attitude, so how do I tell the difference between what's a skill and what's knowledge?" asked Tom.

"There are a couple of ways to highlight the difference." replied The Magician. "First, once you learn a skill, you usually have it for life, whilst knowledge is information often related to your job at a particular point in time. For example, a team leader might need time management skills and good communication skills. Once they've mastered those skills they'll have them for life. But they'll still need to have knowledge such as the systems and procedures the team need to follow and what the objectives are for the team. If they have a break for five years the knowledge they need will probably have changed, but the skills will be broadly the same."

Tom reflected for a moment, then said, "Okay, I can see that so far, but you said there was a second way."

"Yes, the second way of looking at the difference between skills and knowledge is to think of knowledge as the 'what' and skills as the 'how'." The Magician paused then went on. "If you send a new team leader on a time management course they'll be given the knowledge they need to manage time effectively, but that knowledge doesn't make them good time managers. It's only when they understand the knowledge and decide to apply it, that they turn that knowledge into a long-term skill."

There was a moment's silence, then Tom said, "So if I was a doctor, part of my training would be about how to communicate with patients, and assuming I understood and applied that knowledge, I would then have that as a skill."

"That's right."

Tom went on, "So the skill would remain with me whatever type of medical professional I was. I'd still need different types of medical knowledge if I was a GP, or an anaesthetist or a heart surgeon."

"Exactly," said The Magician smiling at Tom.

"That's really helpful. Andrea and I are going to start looking at that right away. We don't want to wait until we've got the new HR manager in place, after all that could take months." He paused, then said, "But the good news is, we've got some first interviews arranged for the end of next week."

The Magician then continued. "The thing to remember here about capability Tom as I just mentioned, is that it's all about application. You could have a person who has all the skill and knowledge you would wish for, but application is down to how engaged they are in the business. If you develop a person so that they want to apply their skills and knowledge, you will always get a better result. When a person feels valued they give that little bit more effort, which can make all the difference between a good result and a great result. The best way to make a person feel valued is by development, coaching and training. When you do that properly everybody wins."

Tom looked concerned "But all that takes time, it's the reason Andrea's been pushing for the HR manager. We haven't really had time to do that development work, is this new HR person we're looking for the right person to take care of that development work?"

The Magician gave Tom a reassuring look. "Certainly the HR manager's role will be to co-ordinate the development of your people, but can you really expect a newcomer to your business to know everything that your people need to learn?"

"No Tom, the development and coaching work will be driven by your leaders and by the Stars in your business. Much of your role will be about developing the capabilities of your senior team, so that they can in turn develop their teams with the help of their Stars."

"I suppose that what your suggesting here is that

development of people is a good way of generating more Stars and potentially pulling the Rebels back on side?" asked Tom.

"That's exactly right!" said The Magician, "So I hope you'll do the profile for the HR and Training Manager role before you start the interviews, to ensure that whoever you choose is right for your business."

"It'd be nice," replied Tom, "But I don't know how we'll find the time."

"If you don't create a profile how will you know you've recruited the best candidate? You've also got to think about your people developers as a whole and what you need from them."

Tom knew The Magician was right, it was just a question of how to find the time with all the sales stuff as well.

"Look," said The Magician handing Tom a piece of paper, "These questions might help."

Developing capability in the business:

Who could be the capability developers in your business?

How could you develop their people development ability?

What attitudes would they need in order to develop people well?

What would need to be important to them in a job for them to successfully develop others?

What would they need in terms of skills?

What would they need in terms of knowledge?

What would they need to be able to do?

What behaviours do you want to see them display consistently?

Concept 4
Capabilities – The things people have learned to do or not do

In Chapter 4, you discover how recognising the different behaviour types can help you as you manage your own teams or organisation. Let's explore the issues highlighted within the chapter.

Andrea – is she a Rebel or not? When Tom speaks to Andrea he takes the time to find out how she is feeling and quickly realises that his own short-comings have contributed to her feeling taken for granted. After their second meeting where various things are agreed to Andrea's satisfaction, she is back to behaving as she usually does – as a Star.

Chris – is he a Rebel in the making, or a Star in waiting? During Tom and Andrea's discussion they talk about Chris and both wonder if they have mis-managed him. Anyone who exhibits strong behaviours of either a Star or a Willing Helper will usually continue to do so unless someone upsets or mis-manages them.

Rory – the unknown? It is obvious from Tom and Andrea's first conversation that both of them have avoided tackling issues with Rory. This is partly because they don't understand his technical specialism and partly because he is not naturally communicative. Once Andrea decided to talk to him, showing an interest in what matters to Rory, she saw a whole different side to him. At the moment he is behaving more like a Fence Sitter than a Rebel, but Andrea can see potential to move him to be more Willing Helper or maybe even a Star. However, under a more negative influence he could easily become more Rebellious.

Terry – the hidden Rebel? Terry's behaviour is probably the hardest to understand. He is displaying typical Rebel behaviour; he is working to his own agenda building up his own business but he is doing it in secret. The one person who doesn't see any of the negative sides to Terry is Tom. This is because Terry is using his excellent communication skills in a manipulative way. There was probably a time in Terry's past where he was badly treated by a leader and so he is now looking after himself and no one else, probably justifying his actions as normal and the right thing to do given that he has just resigned.

Terry almost certainly doesn't see himself as a Rebel, in fact if asked, he would probably see himself as a Star who has been let down 'again'. The fact that Tom is a smart and successful business person and yet he is still caught out by Terry is a sign of how difficult it can be to spot true Rebel behaviour. It is also possible that since Tom recruited Terry and had a positive opinion of him, Tom was blind to Terry's shortcomings, instead only seeing what he wanted to see.

Tom's big problem is time. He has mentioned many times that he hasn't given the time to his team to keep things on track, instead simply assuming that all was OK. Without any data to the contrary, why would he need to change anything? The business was going well, profits were up. Do you remember the analogy of the body at the beginning of the book? Results can be misleading - when the system is out of balance, you will know eventually, as the signals you ignore will just get louder. Tom had all the signals but chose to ignore them. Having more accurate data and listening to it would have saved him a lot of pain! A regular employee survey or frequent team discussions will highlight problems like this.

How to use awareness of behaviours
Observing the behaviours of people as Stars, Rebels, Willing Helpers or Fence Sitters can be a very effective way to gauge what is happening in a team or business and how well people are engaged with their job and the business. They are instant and typically in the moment. This makes them a great tool for any good leader as long as the leader devotes the time to observe people in their natural surroundings. Remember behaviours can change with the situation.

Two secrets for using this tool effectively are firstly, look for the changes. With both Andrea and Chris there had been definite changes in behaviour. Sometimes the changes happen quite quickly, other times they may be more gradual. Being vigilant to any potential changes and talking to your people about the changes you perceive is the earliest warning you have.

Secondly, investigate differences of opinion. So far in the story there have been two main examples of differences of opinion. The most obvious is that Suzie never liked or trusted Terry, and as The Magician pointed out Suzie is usually a good judge of people. Tom dismissed her warning and didn't bother to ask anyone else. When he did start to ask other people, Andrea, Darren and Suja corroborated Suzie with a damning opinion.

The other difference of opinion concerned Suja; she was one of Tom's longest serving staff and he'd always seen her display the behaviour of a Willing Helper. When Tom started hearing a more negative view of her from Terry, it should have sounded a warning. He could have checked why Suja wasn't displaying Willing Helper behaviour any more, or whether Terry was distorting the truth for his own benefit.

Understanding why other leaders or managers have a different view of a person's behaviour will always help you to see the reality more clearly.

Rebels for example often talk negatively about their team members to unconsciously move the focus away from themselves and mask their lack of self-esteem or confidence. Also the ability to blame someone else for the team's lack of performance allows the Rebel to dodge the responsibility to fix things themselves, where they should really be proactive and use their capabilities to tackle the problem. But why should they, if they're disengaged? It's not their problem, right?

It is quite common for Rebels to blame poor performance on their peers or colleagues, often indicating that if it wasn't for them (the Rebel) things would all go horribly wrong. In fact it is also the team members that are actually holding things together, despite the Rebel. The team are probably not getting the recognition for their efforts.

This is where good leadership comes in, seeing the problem for what it is and tapping into the Rebel's capability. Showing them that they can make a difference and feel positive when you give them the appropriate recognition, whilst also recognising the contribution of the whole team.

Capability
The other concept introduced in Chapter 4 is 'capability' – what a person is capable of doing. It is a combination of their skills and knowledge as well as their attitude and behaviour.

The Magician explains the difference between skills and knowledge in two ways. Firstly a skill is something that you usually have for life once you have gained it, while knowledge can be more specific to a particular job and forgotten when not used. Secondly, you can give someone knowledge of what to do. It's only when they actively apply that knowledge repeatedly to develop a skill and then fully engage that capability, that they create consistent behaviour.

To find the best person for a particular role and to use people effectively as part of a team you need to consider the knowledge, skills and attitude required for the role. That's why it is so helpful to prepare a person specification, listing the skills, knowledge and attitude requirements as well as a job description for each role in your organisation.

Attitude
One other element in the story which we haven't explored is that of attitude.

If you've ever managed people you'll know just how important attitude is. You can employ a person with all the required skill and knowledge but the wrong attitude will result in them not wanting to apply that skill or knowledge, therefore restricting their engagement in the business.

As a rule of thumb recruit first for a person with the right attitude – this is really the basis for the behaviour types highlighted in the earlier chapters. Then look for the right skills, knowledge and experience.

A person's attitude is often linked to their values and we find these out by asking what's important to them. For example, if serving customers is important to them, then they will have a positive attitude towards customers.

If teamwork is important to them, they will respond well to a supportive team, and typically contribute to the team and its well-being. The opposite can also be true. When you ask what is important to a person, if teamwork isn't mentioned, then teamwork is less of a priority to them than the other answers, which they gave as 'important'. Logically then, when you interview a person and identify their job values by asking what's important to them about a job or career, you need to listen to what they do say and what they don't list as part of their values. If a critical value is missing, then the likelihood is that learning the corresponding skill wasn't important to them. The probability is that the skill will be missing too, and difficult to train in.

In the first half of this chapter, The Magician gives Tom a task to complete to identify the behaviours of his team members that he wants and doesn't want, by asking a few simple questions:

- Identify, the behaviours you would like to see from the team day-to-day.
- To get those behaviours consistently, what attitudes would need to be present within the team, what would have to be important to them?

- Consider those who may be Fence Sitters or Rebels.
- Consider what different behaviours you would like to see them express, for you to feel like they are more engaged.
- What behaviours would you like to see them stop?
- Consider those who are Stars and Willing Helpers. What behaviours are you getting that you want, and what do you need to do to keep them engaged?

When Andrea identified what was important to Rory, she explored something he had a positive attitude towards; his daughter. She showed him she was interested in something which mattered to him, implying that what he values is important to her as well.

This process of identifying what's important to a person is a great way to generate a positive attitude in the person and identify whether they will 'fit in' with the rest of the team. This process is explained in detail on page 118.

Your task:
Identify the key capabilities you need within your team. Identify the gaps in capability that need to be bridged in order for the team to be capable of the behaviours you want.

Then consider:

Who could be the capability developers in your business?

How could you develop their people development ability?

What attitudes would they need in order to develop people well?

What would need to be important to them in a job for them to successfully develop others?

What would they need in terms of skills?

What would they need in terms of knowledge?

What would they need to be able to do?

What behaviours do you want to see them display consistently as capability developers?

Chapter 5 – Finding a new Star

Late on Monday afternoon…

Tom looked down at the notes he'd made during the day. He'd had a meeting with the whole of the sales team in the morning. It was obvious none of them were disappointed that Terry had left. It was also clear everyone had already heard the news; the grapevine had certainly been buzzing over the weekend. At least that was a positive sign that the team still worked well together.

Once they'd dealt with the practicalities of covering Terry's notably few appointments for the coming weeks, Tom had explained that he would be acting as Head of Sales until they found a replacement. In the meantime, he assured them that things would be managed rather more professionally from now on.

After the meeting, he'd had separate meetings with each member of the team. He suspected that none had the potential to take on Terry's role as Head of Sales. Either they didn't have the skills and knowledge, or they didn't have the right ambition to take on the responsibility.

The more positive news was that as Terry had left, Suja who had been working part-time now wanted to work full-time because her son was settled at school. Tom had wondered if she would take on more of a management role. She certainly had the skills and knowledge, but it was clear that she wanted to put her family first for a few more years.

A knock at the door heralded Tom's last meeting of the day. It was with Simon, the lad who apparently had done much of the work to win their newest client. Tom started the meeting by congratulating him and acknowledging that Simon would now receive the credit that was due to him. Then Tom started to get Simon to talk about himself and what mattered to him.

As the conversation developed Simon said, "Suja says I should be straight with you. I get on well with her and she says you're a really good guy to work for."

"I certainly try to be," replied Tom wondering what was coming next.

"The thing is, you don't know me all that well. I only joined the business about a month before Terry and since then I've hardly done more than say hello to you by the coffee machine." Tom nodded knowing it was true. Simon went on, "The thing is, I want to be like you one day and have my own business. I know I'm not ready for that yet, but I reckon I'm ready to be a Sales Manager. I've got a second interview for a job later this week, but it's up north and my girlfriend and I don't really want to move."

"I see," said Tom still listening carefully, though his mind was turning over possibilities.

"So I wondered if there might be scope for me to be a Sales Manager here, now that Terry's gone. I know I'll need training and it would be great to have someone like you as a mentor. Suja says you taught her everything she knows." He carried on, "I'm keen to learn and I won't let you down if you give me a chance."

Tom looked into the eyes of this keen young man. In a lot of ways Tom felt he was looking at a reflection of how he'd been fifteen or twenty years before. He could see that Simon would want to do his own thing one day, but he could also see Simon had a lot of potential in the meantime, especially as he was being honest with Tom about his ultimate ambitions. They discussed the company's future plans, and Simon's ambitions and goals.

"Let me have a think about that," said Tom drawing the meeting to a close. "I'd certainly be sorry to lose you at the moment. I'll come back to you in a couple of days."

As the door closed behind Simon, Tom's mind was racing ahead with his plans and ideas. He'd almost accepted Simon's suggestion then and there. When he'd been Simon's age he would have done, but he had a little more wisdom these days.

He waited a few minutes then went into the main office.

"You look happy," Andrea said as Tom approached her, "Have you got some good news?"

"I think I might have. If you've got a minute I'll tell you."

She nodded as he looked round and saw that the meeting room was free. They sat down as Tom said proudly, "I think I've found us a new Sales Manager."

"But we haven't even advertised yet, have we?"

"No, but I've just had an interesting conversation with young Simon!" He went on to recount the meeting.

"But he'll need a lot of training and support won't he?"

asked Andrea. "I mean he's a bright young lad, and he's good at his job, but it's a big step from that to a Sales Manager role."

"I know it is, but he's clearly got the potential. If we don't give him the opportunity, somebody else will. He's already got an interview somewhere else. The benefits are he's here, he knows our services, he knows our people and he's really good at selling." Tom went on, "If we recruit externally I'm going to have to give a lot of time to sales until we find someone, and even then it'll take me months to hand everything over, and we might also lose Simon in the process."

"You said it yourself, Andrea," said Tom. "Attitude is key and he certainly has a positive attitude in spades."

"Yes, but can he manage people? That's different." Andrea looked unconvinced.

Tom pressed on "I think he could manage people, he has a lot of the right qualities, and training him would be so easy, he seems to have the right aptitude for it, it seems to be a great opportunity and it would take time to get anyone up to speed, and we'd lose more time recruiting someone we don't know." Tom paused. "One thing" he said "There's also the risk of bringing an unknown person into a management position. We did that with Terry and look where it got us."

"So you're thinking you might as well spend that time training Simon," mused Andrea.

"That's it," replied Tom. "Also, I'm thinking of getting Suja to support him. She could easily do a Sales Manager's job, but she doesn't want the responsibility."

"Would she be happy with that?" asked Andrea. "I mean you'd be using her to train up someone with far less experience than her and 10 years her junior, so that he could be her boss. I saw that where I worked before, and it caused so much resentment."

"I hadn't thought of it quite like that," replied Tom.

"I guess it depends on whether Suja's happy to do it. As much as anything, Tom, it'll be down to how you sell the idea to her," suggested Andrea, "Also, I think we'd have to communicate it really clearly so that everyone knows what's happening and what the intention is."

"We have to be careful here, Tom. Look at what happened with Chris – if you recall we made a decision to promote Zeb because we thought Chris wasn't bothered. In hindsight the promotion of Zeb turned Chris right off and we're only just getting over that. Are you sure that promotion isn't important to Suja? I know she says she doesn't want the responsibility but I'm not sure I'd want to train and develop a person to be as good as me only for them to become my boss, if promotion is important to her, we could give her a development role to support Simon without the sales management responsibility?"

"Ok" said Tom, "I need a conversation with Suja separately. I need to really explore what's important to her to be sure we can maintain her motivation while developing Simon to be Sales Manager. On your way back to your office, Andrea, please ask Suja to pop in and see me."

Suja entered Tom's office much happier than at their last meeting. Tom commented how much lighter she seemed and she agreed. "Thank you for being so understanding when we spoke before", she said. "It's a relief knowing that I can voice my concerns again."

"That's why I wanted a talk," said Tom. "It's been a while since we talked about your career and I'd like to discuss the future." Suja joined Tom at the coffee table.

Tom went through the process of identifying Suja's objectives and values, they discussed Tom's plans for Simon and explored Suja's potential role in supporting Simon's development. Finally, Tom raised the question about Suja developing Simon to eventually become her boss. Suja reassured Tom that she was happy with the situation and that actually Tom's suggestion fitted very well with her domestic life and her family, which were both very important to her.

Later that evening…

Tom stood in the open park area looking out to the horizon whilst Barney had his final run around before bedtime. It was getting late; he'd been talking to Suzie at length about his plans for Simon. After all the ideas that had been buzzing around his head Tom noticed the contrast with the still of the night sky.

He gazed up at the twinkling stars, the Great Bear overhead just starting to be visible as the clouds cleared, lost for a moment in thoughts of space and the universe. He only gradually became aware of The Magician walking towards him. As they stood side-by-side Tom said, "I do remember what you told me about giving myself time to be still and listen to the quiet voice inside me."

"And do you do it?"

"Oh yes," replied Tom. "I do it. But not always as much as I should. The good thing is I'm getting better at realising when I'm not doing it. Then I make some space for myself and let my unconscious mind come up with the answers."

The Magician asked, "Is that what you're doing now?"

"Yes, yes, I think it is," replied Tom a little hesitantly. "The thing is I think I've found a trainee Sales Manager. Not someone to take over at Terry's level, but one of the existing team who's really keen to progress – a young man called Simon."

"And has this young man got the right knowledge, skills and attitude?"

"I'm sure he's got the right attitude and I know I can train him in terms of skills and knowledge. I'd still need to be quite hands on in terms of sales, but in a lot of ways it makes sense at the moment." Tom paused then went on, "The thing is I want to make sure I get it right this time. The sales pipeline's in such a poor state I can't afford to spend months training Simon for him to decide to leave, or to realise he's just not up to the job."

"In that case you need to make sure you have the right systems in place to support him," said The Magician.

"We put sales systems in place three years ago, but they don't seem to have helped very much. Terry just used them to focus on short-term sales to maximise his Christmas bonus – how I wish I hadn't paid him that. Anyway, he obviously wasn't encouraging the team to take a long-term view."

"Tom, you need to remember that things change. The

systems you put in place when you only employed 12 people and you and Suja were the whole of the sales team won't work for the sort of business you have today."

"When you put it like that, I suppose it's pretty obvious," Tom replied dejectedly.

"Don't beat yourself up too much. Just remember businesses change gradually day by day, and we don't always see those changes. So every now and then you need to check that your systems and procedures are still fit for purpose."

"So maybe we ought to look at the holiday system too as that was the trigger that caused Andrea to think of leaving."

"Exactly," replied The Magician. "But for now let's focus on the systems to support Simon."

Tom interjected, "Oh they're okay now. I can get Simon to look at the sales system and come to me with his recommendations. If I get him to do it jointly with Suja I'm sure they'll work out just what we need."

"But Tom, what about the other systems Simon will need? I don't just mean the IT systems."

Tom looked puzzled, "Like what?"

The Magician continued "Like all the other processes and procedures, systems and protocols that help you to ensure that your people do what you need them to do, and don't do what you don't want them to do. I mean things like training, remuneration, reward and recognition, as well as how the team communicates and how frequently, and how you share progress with the team. There are all sorts of systems that you need to put in place since you've grown the business."

"Well I've at least started thinking about how we'll train him," replied Tom.

"Tom, that's absolutely great, but for example have you thought about whether you'll take the team meeting or whether he will? Have you thought about whether the team should be set individual targets or team targets?"

"Hold on a minute," interrupted Tom suddenly realising that he was getting cold and that Barney was acting like he wanted to go home. "I think what you're saying is that there's a lot to consider, but it is all stuff I know about. I just need to take time to set it up properly right from the start. I also clearly need to do it with Simon and Suja so it's their systems and processes that meet the needs of today, not what I would have done three years ago."

"That's about it," said The Magician. Then he reached into his coat pocket and pulled out a piece of paper. As he handed it to Tom he said, "These questions might help when you're thinking about your systems and processes."

Tom glanced down at the questions. When he looked up he realised he was alone again with his thoughts and the stars.

Consider your team or organisation

What are the behaviours and actions you want to encourage or discourage?

What systems can you put in place to encourage or discourage those behaviours and actions?

What systems can you put in place to measure those behaviours and actions?

Here are some pointers:

Communication/sharing information/ customer data/company data.

Business results – sales turnover/profit – measuring, rewarding, managing.

Training and development – measuring training needs, bridging gaps, continuous improvement.

Team working – Team rules/ways of working.

Operational procedures – completing tasks/audit processes/quality/safety.

Concept 5
Systems and procedures – ways to encourage behaviours and actions you want and discourage behaviours and actions you don't want

Chapter 5 is about how to bring out the best behaviour and support a potential Star or Willing Helper, which means more than just encouragement from their leader.

Tom has discovered that Simon appears to have the potential to be a Star. He has checked his opinion with Andrea and Suja, because they are people who share his values. He trusts they will speak honestly about their experience of Simon and Simon's behaviour.

In his discussion with Andrea, Tom recognises that promoting someone as junior as Simon could cause tensions and resentment. Andrea also warns him of the dangers of using Suja to train Simon and then making him her boss. All this shows how small changes in roles and responsibilities have the potential to turn existing Fence Sitters or Willing Helpers into Rebels as well as Stars.

Teams and organisations are always changing. It's how you handle the changes that matter, not how you avoid them.

Systems and procedures
The opportunity to train Simon as Sales Manager is also the time for Tom to think about the systems and procedures that will support not just Simon but the whole

sales team. This will include training, communication systems and targets as well as IT or operational systems.

When improving employee engagement, communication is often the most important area to focus on. It must be two-way and frequent so having multiple routes is vital. A quick 'stand up' team meeting every day for example might be the way to set the team up with clear priorities and focus.

Tom's business has grown very rapidly in the last few years. The systems he put in place three years ago would not necessarily be effective for the business today. This is very common in small businesses when much of the relevant information is passed on informally as people interact through the day. As a business gets bigger, communication updates must be more formalised and structured, otherwise leaders lose contact with the pulse of the business.

In this chapter, Tom shows his maturity as a leader when he recognises that Simon and Suja should be the people to design the systems they need now. There are two reasons for this. Firstly, they deal with sales everyday now and so know what will help them the most. Secondly, they will feel like they own the systems and will want them to work. Tom can also help them to see that no system will ever remain perfect forever, everything changes and so the wise leader will always be reviewing support systems to see when they need to be refreshed or changed. Tom will also need to ensure that they heed the lessons he's learned from the situation with Terry and the guidance of his mentor, The Magician.

The most important thing about any system is that it promotes the behaviour you want to see in the team or organisation. Systems are an absolutely critical aspect of generating the environment and results which you want. The key distinction here is that the *systems and processes you put in place* will have a deeper effect than training or coaching which we covered within the capability section.

To illustrate with an example: one of the tools we can use to drive behaviour is reward. If we reward employees for exhibiting certain behaviours then they are most likely to be the behaviours we get. Tom fell into the trap of rewarding Terry for short-term sales at the cost of long-term business generation, so he got…short-term sales!

One of the truths of life is that people follow the reward, whether that be, praise or money. If you train a person to do one thing, and then reward them for doing another – well, we know the likely consequence! This is exactly why the culture diagram has the systems and processes circle inside the capabilities circle. Systems and processes will directly influence what people learn to do. The circles behave like a hierarchy, the further into the diagram the circles sit, the more power of influence they have.

Tom may have verbally encouraged Terry to keep generating long-term business, or even just assumed that Terry would be doing that because Tom would do it that way. Terry acted on the short-term reward because the reward system encouraged it and the management system – or absence of it – failed to encourage or ensure long-term business generation. Tom admitted that he had 'left Terry to it', which doesn't sound like much of a monitoring system!

This highlights the truism that if you can't measure it, you can't manage it! If Tom didn't put any system in place to measure long-term business generation activity, he wouldn't know that it wasn't being done. Also if you measure a behaviour and result and ask your team to report it, they think it's important and so they tend to focus on the behaviour or result you are measuring.

A word of caution here. Be careful not to overload your organisation with systems and processes for everything. You will simply have people doing 'systems' things rather than their actual job, this can lead to duplication of tasks and wasting time because people focus on following the procedure rather than delivering outcomes.

One of the reasons Terry took the short-term rather than the long-term approach was a fundamental misalignment of values between himself and Tom's business. He was following his own selfish ends. This meant he was plain and simply the wrong person for the job by virtue of his misaligned values, and this expressed itself in his behaviour and attitude. He clearly had the right skills and knowledge for the job, but didn't do the right things because those 'right things' weren't important to him; hence he was undoubtedly a 'Rebel'.

The lesson to learn here is that sometimes, even if you have the right systems, the 'wrong' person will find his or her way round them to meet their own ends. What you need then are measurement systems to catch them quickly, and this is what Tom didn't do, he simply left Terry to get on with things. An even better solution of course would be to recruit the right people in the first place, based on values and attitude, but as we saw with Tom, he did think that he had recruited the right person.

Ideally you want to keep systems to a minimum, just enough to ensure your people do the right things. You also need to allow for growth. If you're having to overload your organisation with systems, you probably have the wrong people leading and/or low levels of employee engagement.

So what kind of systems should you have in place? In simple terms you want systems which encourage people to do what you want them to do. The systems you use could be rewards or procedures, regular interaction, or simply ways of operation. Ideally the systems should encourage the right behaviour <u>and</u> allow you to monitor progress.

Here are some examples of good operational systems and procedures:

- If you want a team to work together and share information then set up a regular interaction for the team, maybe a team meeting or conference call.
- If you want a debt to be recovered efficiently and the people concerned to do the job well, create a system of step-by-step actions which you have proven work over time for them to follow.
- If you want the sales team to focus on profitability rather than just sales revenue, then reward them based on gross margin rather than pure sales revenue. I've seen sales people discount too far to get a sale because their reward system didn't penalise them for an unprofitable sale!
- If you want people to pay attention to certain target objectives or key performance indicators (KPIs) which you have set, then you need to regularly communicate progress towards those targets or KPIs, probably on a whiteboard or similar visual system which people can see all the time, and you would need to meet with the team to review results on the whiteboard and agree actions every day, week, or month.

Your task
Consider the regular behaviours and outcomes you want in your business organisation or team and list them

specifically. This is probably best done by the relevant section of the team or business. As a hint, consider what your best Stars do day-to-day as the place to start.

Consider systematic ways of encouraging these behaviours or discouraging their opposite. See how many creative ways you could do this. Ask other people for suggestions.

Consider systems of reward, systems of measurement, and systems of procedure.

In working on this task consider all possible options, be creative and where practical involve the team in the creation of those systems as it encourages ownership. Ask the team to outline the way they do things now, then identify where the measurements should be.

What I've found works very well is to map out the enquiry or order journey from beginning to end highlighting each stage of the journey, what happens at each stage, the inputs and outputs and who's involved. Be prepared to challenge items in the process; is it really necessary? Also identify where a step has been adapted by an individual based on their own specialist knowledge despite a fault in the system. Unfortunately, you may not find out about this until they are off work or on holiday.

People clearly need a say in the processes they create and follow, but the processes should also be able to be replicated by others in case the key person leaves or is off work.

For each key step in the process, identify a measure of completion for that step, and you can then consider if the data is available to make this measure a regular KPI. For example, let's say that a company makes widgets – one of the key steps on the order journey is the shipping of the widget. If you agree a delivery date with a client, then you will need data to confirm that the widget was shipped on time. Your system should therefore register the agreed delivery date, the actual delivery date and compare the two. You can then report this information back to the rest of the team – x% of our widgets have been delivered on time in full (OTIF). A target can then be set for the team to keep achieving their OTIF KPI.

Chapter 6 – Reviewing the direction re-engaging the team

Late Friday afternoon…

"I can't believe none of them are suitable," said Tom staring into his mug of tea.

"I know," replied Andrea. "They all looked really good on paper, but their attitudes… None of them came across as being Willing Helpers, never mind Stars; they were only interested in the pay, promotions and prospects! I'd been looking forward to handing over the HR and training stuff, but frankly if we appointed any of them it would just cause more problems in the long-run."

Tom reflected for a moment, then perked up a little as he said, "It would have been a bit exceptional if we'd found two new managers in a week. The good news is Simon and Suja are working really well together. He's full of bright ideas, and to be honest I'm quite enjoying being more involved with sales again."

"How are the rest of the sales team responding to the change?"

"So far it's going fine. Some of them know they didn't want the role, but the two who were interested are taking it a bit harder. It's just something we'll have to manage and it's good experience for Simon," replied Tom. Then he asked, "How are you getting on with Rory? Have you turned him into a Star yet?"

"Give me a chance," snapped Andrea. Then she saw Tom grinning at her and realised he was joking. "It's a real case of two steps forward and one step back at the moment. I've found that buried deep beneath that dour exterior there's actually a wicked sense of humour; that's the positive revelation of the week."

"And the negative?" asked Tom.

"He really doesn't like dealing with people."

"You seem to be doing all right," observed Tom wryly.

"Yes, I know," Andrea replied with a sigh. "I think that's because I'm making the effort and showing an interest in him. But the reason he's so good at what he does is because he prefers dealing with machines, rather than people."

"Well isn't that okay?" asked Tom. "After all, it's what we pay him to do."

"It is and it isn't. It's great in terms of doing a good job for the work that comes to us. But you won't be so happy when you learn we could be doing five or even ten times as much work in his area."

"What!" exclaimed Tom.

"The more I'm talking to him, the more I can see there are masses of missed opportunities to offer customers more of our services, especially the work Rory does."

"Why didn't he say?"

"Firstly, his people skills aren't brilliant so he didn't take the time to understand other needs that our clients might have, and secondly nobody asked him. He was simply left to get on with the job, so he assumed no one was interested and didn't want to cause extra work he couldn't cope with. I can see how we thought he was a Rebel but his lack of engagement is our fault not his."

Tom groaned.

"Look on the bright side," said Andrea. "At least we know now and I have a cunning plan to sort it out for the future."

"How are you going to do that?"

"I figured we may as well use the strengths that we have, so I've moved Chris over to work with Rory permanently. The plan is they'll work together as a team with Chris dealing with the customers, which is what he enjoys, and Rory working on the machines, which is what he likes. I think it will mean we get a lot more work and can start to grow that team even more in time."

"You really think there's that much work?" questioned Tom.

"Definitely. I also want to re-organise the rest of the operational teams a bit. I'm still finalising the details but I'll talk it through with you soon to see if you agree."

"Andrea, you've no need to talk it through with me. Operations is your side, you do what you need to do," said Tom. "I've enough to look after with sales and finance."

"No Tom, I'd value a second opinion, and we've always talked things through before when I've reorganised my lot. It's the lack of regular discussion which started all these problems. Anyway I don't think I'll do anything until we've appointed the HR person and I can say goodbye to all that."

"I'll get onto the recruitment company on Monday," said Tom making a note to himself.

"Good," said Andrea gathering her things together. "As far as I'm concerned, the sooner we have a separate HR Manager who can report to you the better."

Sunday afternoon…

Tom sat on the familiar bench outside the sailing club. Two things had been niggling away at him all weekend. When Suzie's mum had suggested that the family go to the cinema, he'd seen the opportunity to allow them to enjoy themselves while he took a bit of time out to reflect.

He waited patiently knowing he needed to relax and be still. He watched the gulls wheeling, followed the lapping of the waves and had just begun to be aware that the stones on the beach were different colours, when, sure enough, a few moments later The Magician walked along the path towards him.

"What's been troubling you my friend?" asked the older man.

Tom stared out to sea for a minute, not really sure what to say. Eventually he replied, "It's nothing major, it's silly really, but two little things are bugging me. It's as though that quiet voice inside is trying to tell me that they're bigger issues than I realise."

"So what are these little issues that might be bigger issues?"

"The first one is that Simon didn't know anything about our vision and values. Obviously I've told him now and we're going to remind the rest of the team at the weekly meeting on Monday. The thing is, I know I told Terry so I don't understand why he didn't keep reinforcing them with his team. I guess that was an issue with Terry and as he's gone I've tried to dismiss it, but it keeps coming back to me."

"So is your concern about delegation?" asked The Magician.

"My concern is around why Terry didn't share our vision and values and do what I told him."

"Exactly my point," replied his mentor. "When you delegate something it doesn't mean your involvement stops. You still need to have some sort of checking process in place to make sure it's happening. You can delegate responsibility for any task but ultimately you're still accountable for it. Well, that's assuming you're still the Managing Director."

"But I'd be constantly checking up on people. I might as well do it all myself," snapped Tom.

The Magician didn't respond for a moment. Then he said, "The key Tom is to have people fully engaged, but more on that later, so what's the other issue?"

"Oh, that's just who the new manager reports to."

"What do you mean?" asked The Magician.

"Well, I'd assumed they'd report to Andrea, but from something she said on Friday, I think she's expecting them to report to me just like the other managers."

"I see," said The Magician quietly.

"What do you see," asked Tom.

"I see why the quiet voice inside you is telling you these issues are bigger than you think." He paused then went on, "Tom, what do you perceive is the root cause of the problems you've discovered over the last few weeks?"

"Well, Terry mainly."

"But how did Terry manage to do so much damage for so long without you knowing? That quiet voice inside is trying to tell you that all these issues are symptoms of a problem with the leadership in your business."

Tom stared out to sea, then said, "But I'm the leader in my business."

"So you are, so you are," said The Magician quietly. He paused as this sank in and Tom grasped the implications. "There are two things you need to consider here Tom. Firstly, the business is of a size that you need some way of making sure that things are on track, that you are achieving your goals and that the team are fully engaged so that you can keep achieving your goals. We talked about this when we discussed systems and processes so you need to look at some way of checking and maintaining the level of staff engagement. Perhaps an employee feedback mechanism so you know quickly if people are disengaging."

"That sounds complicated" complained Tom, "I've already got a lot on my plate without looking after every employee!"

"That's where the second item comes into play" said The Magician. "You can't be expected to keep tabs on every employee, you need to make sure your leaders are doing that well. Maybe now that the business is so much bigger you need a new leadership structure to deliver the vision and values which you were so keen to explain to Simon."

"But I've got a management team" said Tom, "Ingrid for finance and IT; we'll get someone for HR and Training, Simon's gradually taking on the sales management, and then of course there's Andrea managing all the operational side."

"I know all about your management team, Tom. It's you who sets the direction and delegates the management to the team. It's they who manage the day-to-day running of the business."

"That's right," said Tom.

The Magician continued. "The problem is, with sixty people looking to you for leadership, on the one hand you haven't got time to check that your managers are managing in the way you want them to, but you still need to be aware of the whole team and how well they are engaged in the business by you and your management team. The situation with Terry is a classic example of you not having the information to tell you that things were going off track. You've admitted yourself Tom that you had no idea what was happening with the sales team. You trusted Terry and left him to it. And look at the mess that's got you into."

"But I can't do everything."

"That's my point Tom. There are two things to consider here. What needs to expand is the leadership structure and you need to have some way of getting a regular understanding of the team and how well they are engaged. Firstly let's talk about the leadership structure. So the question is, do any of your existing managers have the potential to take on more of a leadership role, which means less doing the day-to-day stuff, and more of setting and communicating the vision?"

Tom said immediately, "Ingrid's great at what she does, but she's a real introvert and there's no way I could call her a leader, she's a very good manager though. So the only other one is Andrea and I already think of her as a leader."

"OK, so what's the difference between Andrea and Ingrid?" asked The Magician.

Tom looked puzzled, "How do you mean?"

"You said that Andrea is already a leader. What makes you say that?" asked The Magician.

"Well, she gets things done, makes decisions, makes things happen, I can rely on her!" Tom seemed almost frustrated at the question.

"Ah" said The Magician, "So she already has the mindset of a leader? What about the position of a leader, does she have that too?"

"Well she's a manager in the business if that's what you mean" said Tom still confused.

"But does she see herself as a leader of the business?" asked The Magician. "Does she have the authority to be a leader like you? Do the staff see her as one?"

"I've never really thought about it, I've kind of assumed she already is but we've not formally agreed to it" said Tom, now finally beginning to grasp the point.

The Magician stayed silent giving Tom time to think. Finally Tom said, "Do you mean make Andrea a Director and get someone else as Operations Manager?"

"Would that work?" asked The Magician.

"In a lot of ways I treat her as my co-director already, especially now we've gone back to working more closely together like we did before Terry arrived." Tom went on, "But she probably doesn't think of herself that way and nor do the rest of the staff, although I'm sure her team take more notice of her than they do of me. The thing is, we couldn't afford to take on an Operations Manager as well and I don't think there'd be enough for Andrea to do."

"So maybe you could consider making Andrea Operations Director?" suggested his mentor.

Tom thought about the idea. "I could have the structure set up so that the HR and Training Manager reports to her. At the same time Andrea stays as Operations Manager until the business has grown a bit more, then we'd be ready to appoint a new Ops Manager. Andrea knows the job so well it would be easy for her to check that things keep running smoothly."

"What about support for Andrea" asked The Magician?

"Well," said Tom, "in the meantime we can strengthen the admin team around Andrea. That way we'll be developing some of her people and giving Andrea time to look at more strategic stuff with me."

The Magician nodded in agreement then said, "Now let's think a little more about the strategic stuff."

"What about it?" asked Tom, puzzled.

"Tom, when was the last time you really reviewed your direction and vision and values?"

"Not since the last time I did it with you," admitted Tom. "But I've been clear about what we've been doing and until now we've stayed pretty much on track."

"But what about your employees Tom, do they all understand and connect with your direction, vision and values? Do they understand it and are they engaged with it?"

"Well I think so." Said Tom "But now you're asking me, and with the trouble we've discovered recently I'm not entirely sure!"

"Good, so I think now is an ideal time for you to review it with your management team, re-connect the team with it and put a process in place so it's reviewed and communicated regularly in the future."

"So do you mean Andrea and I should consider our strategy together, and then work with the whole management team to develop the plans before we communicate it to the rest of the staff?"

"What do you think Tom" asked The Magician "how could that work in practice?"

"It would certainly promote greater ownership for Andrea. Then she and I could check that everything the business is doing is aligned with the vision and values, but as long as we're both clear on the direction and keep it in mind we should soon spot anything that deviates."

"How do you feel about this approach Tom?" asked The Magician.

"It feels OK" replied Tom. "It would feel like Andrea and I are working more as a team, and that we'd be involving the management team in our overall strategy, which has to be good."

"So, let me just get this straight in my mind," said Tom. "You're suggesting Andrea and I each have two roles in the business. We'll both be leaders in our roles as directors and we'll each keep a management role at the moment: sales for me and operations for Andrea." The Magician nodded as Tom went on, "But if the business keeps growing, ultimately we'll have other people in those management roles."

"Yes, assuming you and Andrea decide the time is right for the business to grow. That's all part of reviewing your direction. Think of it as being a part-time leader role and part-time manager role."

Tom looked concerned, "But Andrea's already complaining

about having too much on."

"That's why you're recruiting another manager Tom, to release some of Andrea's time," reassured The Magician.

When we started talking a few weeks ago you said Stars were leaders, so what about the other Stars in the business? You're surely not saying they should be directors?" queried Tom.

The Magician laughed. "No, certainly not, although some of them, like Simon, might have potential in the future. No most Stars are the people who have the skills to lead and inspire the people who work around them. They're the informal leaders, they have leadership qualities without necessarily being in formal leadership roles. Remember that leadership is not necessarily positional, a person can be a positive role model for others without being in a formal leadership role. It's their mindset that sets them apart from the rest. Whatever role they're in, they tend to think like leaders. They're the ones who will help the directors and managers turn Fence Sitters into Willing Helpers. But to do it they need clear direction from you and Andrea. Stars need to be valued and respected, given opportunities to shine and develop themselves, that's what leadership is all about. It's your job to help those Stars to shine."

"So what about Terry? Where did he fit into all this?" asked Tom.

"Not all leaders are true Stars, though they can seem like them. Terry had the leadership position because you gave him the leader role, arguably before he'd earned it, and you treated him as a leader. Everyone knew that you thought he was great but he didn't have the leadership mindset, he didn't develop abilities in others, he didn't create, he just took. That was the difference with Terry. He was never really a Star, and he certainly became a Rebel. As you saw, his team finally turned on him because he didn't lead or develop them."

"I get it," said Tom. "And I guess one of the things Andrea and I should always be looking out for is anyone who might turn into a Rebel. Then it's up to us to work with them to see if we can turn them round or help them to see it's time to move on."

"Do you think I could have stopped that happening, Terry becoming more rebellious I mean?" asked Tom.

"It's difficult to say Tom" replied The Magician, "do you think you were reinforcing your leadership message enough, loud enough, and frequently enough? What I call banging the drum?"

"Probably not" said Tom. "I guess I just assumed that Terry would bang the drum for me, and that people already knew the leadership message. How many times do you need to bang the drum? It seems that as the business gets bigger, I have to bang the drum louder and more frequently."

"Well, this ties in with my second point about you having more information available about the work climate and whether your staff are fully engaged. Let's face it Tom, if you had that kind of information about the business, you'd have spotted the problems with Terry a long time ago."

"So how do you suggest I do that, checking with 60

people all the time would be difficult for them and me?" said Tom looking concerned.

"Well, yes and no Tom. There are plenty of ways to get feedback from your teams to gain a real understanding of what's going on. Your people need the opportunity to tell you how they feel, what's working, and what isn't, and they can't always do that in team meetings. Some people find it difficult to raise their concerns, particularly when other people are listening. The leaders and managers in the business are an important part of your business communication. They are your eyes and ears within the workplace, but what if like Terry, they don't tell you what's really going on, or in fact they're part of the problem? The team behind them will feel cut off and begin to disengage, just like your sales team was in danger of doing. You could have lost some good people if you hadn't found out about Terry," The Magician paused.

Tom nodded, thinking carefully about what The Magician had just said. "I see now why involving the managers and then our employees in a discussion about our direction is so important, but how do you get that reliable data if, as you've highlighted, some people don't talk as openly?"

"My suggestion Tom, is that you use some form of regular anonymous survey for all employees to have a say. It doesn't have to be complicated, and it will probably be the first step your new HR manager suggests when he or she is appointed. As I said to you years ago, Tom, it's all a question of balance. Every business will have its share of Stars, Willing Helpers, Fence Sitters and Rebels. The wise leaders are the ones who recognise that the balance is always shifting and respond accordingly, and yes you're right, as the business gets bigger, you need to communicate the leadership message - banging the drum - more frequently. Also, if you want people to be properly engaged you'll need to check that the communication is working."

As usual The Magician reached into his coat pocket and pulled out a piece of paper. As he handed it to Tom he said, "These questions might help as reminder"

As usual The Magician just slipped away, leaving Tom to look over the questions and consider the answers already forming in his head.

Questions from TM:

Do the teams know and understand the business direction and their part in it?

Do the teams know the business values and what's important?

Do you know what's important to them, and are you using their strengths?

Is everyone fully engaged?

Are the leaders fully aligned?

How do you know?

Concept 6
Aligning the team by aligning values and tapping into built-in motivation

In Chapter 6 Andrea displays for us ways she was able to align values within the team. Her work with Rory and Chris begins to show how understanding more about a person helps a good leader to use a person's skills and knowledge to meet a need in the organisation. Andrea now understands Rory's preference for working with machines and Chris' love of chatting to people. By focusing their roles on the things they enjoy and are good at, both Rory and Chris are well on the way to behaving as Willing Helpers. Andrea also shows the commercial acumen of a Star by discovering that there are many opportunities to expand this part of the business. What Andrea has done here is gain a deeper understanding of the people in her team and how she can engage them more successfully.

This brings us to questions around encouraging a person to move from Rebel or Fence Sitter to Star. Is it even possible or are they just 'types' of people? My belief is there is a potential Star in everyone, but that doesn't mean it's easy to bring the Star out into the open. Yet again there's a question of balance – balancing the time and effort it takes to convert a person behaving like a Rebel or Fence Sitter to a Star with the potential benefit to the team or organisation. It can be done, and it's up to you to decide whether it's worth the effort on a case by case basis.

How do you convert Fence Sitters to Willing Helpers and Stars?

As discussed earlier, it's about identifying what motivates or demotivates a person – this is directly connected to a person's values. Values are personal and subjective, affected by our innate aptitude, up-bringing, successes, failures and opinions of people we admire or relate to, and the people we mix with. The vast majority (around 80%) of a person's natural motivation, is linked to their top 4 or 5 values for that context. So, for example most of a person's motivation for doing a job is based around their top 4 or 5 values for a 'job'. We touched on this in chapter 4 when looking to understand attitudes. Attitudes are an outward expression of values. If a person has teamwork in their values, they are likely to have a positive attitude towards teamwork, or indeed be negative toward any team member who doesn't meet his expectations of teamwork.

Our task as a leader is to identify the values of each member of the team and then connect the person's values to what's important to you or your team.

So, how do you identify values? A series of simple but powerful questions will provide this information. In a comfortable and non-threatening environment, ask each team member, ensuring they are calm and relaxed, to answer this question:

- What's important to you about…(add the context here)?

The context could be work related or family or life values. Let's assume you want a person's values for job or career, so you ask "What's important to you about a job or career?" Whatever answer you get, you ask "and what else is important to you about a job or career?" Keep going with the second question until the person runs out of answers.

The list of answers you get is a starting point. For each answer they have given ask "what do you mean by… (the value they gave you)?" The reason we ask this, is that different people can give different meaning to the same words.

Let me illustrate with an example from a client. I asked her what was important in the context of a job or career. She answered amongst others, "job satisfaction". I asked what she meant by job satisfaction, and she said, "To feel I've done my best and made an impact". I then asked, "How would you know you'd made an impact?." She replied, "I can see it and someone tells me."

In the light of this information how would we engage her in a job? The answer is very simple.

- Make sure she's doing something where she can do to her best.
- Make sure she can make an impact.
- Make sure she sees the impact she's making by pointing it out using praise or reward.

We need to identify the top four or five values for a person in the context with which we are working. We need to find out what they mean by each value by asking them how they would know they had that value, and why it's important to them. Why the top four or five values? Because that's where the bulk of a person's motivation can be found, so once you have a list of values, you then ask them to highlight their top five.

Remember, values change over time and a value *not met* over a period of time has a habit of becoming even more important. Equally, a value consistently met can often become less important, almost a 'given'.

There is an additional question you might like to add which is:

"If you had a job which gave you all the values you've mentioned, what would cause you to disengage from or leave that job?" To this question you may get another value or you may get 'nothing'. If you get another value, this is the one you definitely wouldn't want to break if you want to keep the person in your employ!

So let's get back to converting Fence Sitters to Stars. A person will tend to become more Star-like if their values in their work context are being met. Logically then, you need to identify the person's values and either meet them or at least agree that you can't. Some people are happy to accept that a value isn't going to be met for the time being, so it ceases to be an expectation, though it is likely that the value will surface again later. If you can't meet the value and never could, then you may need to concur that it's time for both parties to move on.

One aspect to bear in mind here, is that the process of converting someone to behave like a Star can take time. If a person has been in a situation where their values have not been met for a lengthy period, they will probably be cynical and the time and energy needed to invest may not be worth the return.

Now, imagine you've had a conversation with a member of your team and identified their values. You need to explore together how you could meet their values, but both parties may need to compromise a little here. It's about negotiation. Often it's the simplest things which make the biggest difference. A 'thank you' here, a 'well done' there, bit-by-bit you engage the person such that they want to do more, maybe take risks, or take the initiative. Perhaps they even become more willing to help. Here is the process of a person moving from Fence Sitter to Willing Helper! One point worthy of note here is that setting clear boundaries of what is OK and what is not OK behaviour, and then keeping to those boundaries is an important part of the process.

So what about turning round the Rebel, do we use the same process? Yes we do, it's just that the Rebel is likely to be more cynical and take more time if they've been a Rebel for a while. A Rebel can quickly change back to a Star if you catch them in time, just as we saw with Andrea in the story. Equally, a person who has a lot of time invested in being like a Rebel, and is not open to conversion, is probably better off somewhere else where they can make a fresh start, and moving them on is good for you and them.

The overall key to individual employee engagement is finding out what's important, deciding who could be converted, who can't and acting accordingly.

Another point worthy of note, is that as you review the values of the members of your team, you may begin to see patterns emerging. As highlighted earlier, values are personal and subjective, they have also evolved as part of a person's upbringing. People of a similar age tend to have similar values.

To illustrate using an example: I get a lot of questions from managers about the necessity to give praise. Some managers really struggle with this. The group of people referred to as Millennials tend to value regular recognition and praise. The problem is that many older managers never had this, and so don't understand their need for praise. Imagine what happens to employee engagement when you have a manager managing a Millennial without understanding this value difference. The Millennial expects and responds well to praise. They will disengage from work over time unless the manager, who at this stage doesn't understand the necessity for praise, delivers regular praise and recognition.

Group values evolve over time. We are now seeing that greater numbers of potential employees are more attracted to a role within an organisation which has clarity of vision and purpose than they are attracted to the money or status of a role. So, if you wanted to attract good people from this group, you would need to make sure your purpose, vision and values are clear and attractive.

A Star Leader

This then takes us neatly onto the final crucial aspect which Tom and The Magician discuss, leadership. The way a leader behaves is the largest single factor that contributes to how individual team members also behave.

Remember the concentric circles diagram which showed us how behaviour is encouraged within a team. The circle for leadership sits deeper inside the diagram than the circle for systems or processes. This shows that leadership will probably have a greater effect on behaviour than systems or processes.

So for example if in your business, you have a system of reward which encourages one form of behaviour but a person perceived as a leader gives an instruction to do something different, then the leader's instruction will probably carry. Logically this makes sense because it provides the business with flexibility when facing circumstances, which the systems weren't built to accommodate. But what if the leader happens to be more of a Rebel or is inconsistent in their decisions? There needs to be a benchmark or standard to which the business works in order to make consistent decisions. This benchmark is the vision and values of the business. Teams need clear leadership and it is often the absence of leadership or inconsistent leadership which cause the most problems and the most damage to employee engagement. You may have heard the phrase which illustrates this – *"people don't leave jobs, they leave people and bosses."*

What Tom discovered as he reflected with The Magician was that his lack of clear leadership allowed many of the problems to occur in the first place; though they were also exacerbated by other issues such as poorly defined capabilities and out of date systems and procedures.

Remember that the organisation or team behaves as a system, and each part of that system will depend on the next part to work well. To link back to the team identity model, the inner circles drive the outer circles, and in this respect the model behaves like a hierarchy. The outer circles also affect the inner circles and to make the team work well and deliver outstanding performance, then all the circles must be aligned.

Let me illustrate with an example from personal experience:

I used a residential conference venue in the Midlands where the service was outstanding, the staff were courteous and consistently professional at all times, so I was curious about how in this particular hotel they managed to achieve such outstanding service. Interestingly, I had chosen the venue for a course I was delivering on leadership and personal effectiveness, so the delegates attending were on high alert for anything inconsistent, and were also thoroughly impressed.

When I arrived, the reception and door staff recognised me and addressed me by name, which was a shock as it was the first time I'd stayed at the venue, yet somehow they knew who I was on sight. Throughout the three days the staff repeatedly remembered my name and used the names of all the delegates when they addressed them. The bar staff remembered the drinks our client group had so if we wanted more they could simply replenish them without asking us to remind them what we wanted. The venue staff knew the timings for my session, the equipment set-up, and how they could support it. You'd be surprised how many venues can't even get this right! The service was so outstanding that the delegates decided to buy, sign and present a thank-you card to as many of the staff as they could. Interestingly the venue manager made sure that as many of the staff as possible were there to receive the card when we presented it, and it was the staff who received the card from us, not the manager.

I asked to have a meeting with the venue manager to understand just how he achieved such outstanding service levels. This is how he explained it to me. "We have a set of values which we as a team agree to. Every morning each team leader has a meeting with his/her team to discuss how during the previous day each team member was able to express those values in their work. The team are required to cite at least one example each of how they had *surprised and delighted* a guest by their level of service." You might have guessed, the value they were expressing was, 'We offer surprise and delight!' The 'communication system' of meeting each morning to discuss what happened the previous day was designed to reinforce that value within the team; such that eventually they identified with the value – it became part of their team identity and how they worked.

Let's look at how they 'engineered' *surprise and delight* into the workplace:

- The reception desk and door staff had a photograph of my car taken from their CCTV system on my first exploratory visit so that when I arrived they could 'recognise' me (the value of surprise, facilitated by a system of capturing my image, and encouraging people to recognise me on arrival).
- The bar staff had a table plan showing who sat where and what they were drinking so they could remember and match the appropriate drink to the appropriate person. Simple but very effective.
- The staff involved in my meeting **all** had a copy of my schedule, the equipment needed and how it was to be set out – they asked me for this during my initial meeting when I was selecting the venue.
- The venue provided name badges for every delegate, which allowed them to address every delegate by their first name.

These are all simple systems, which the hotel had put in place to embed the culture and drive the right standards of behaviour, which impacted on the customer experience. They were simple to implement and made a huge difference.

For me the most incredible example, which illustrates just what can happen when employee engagement is really high is this:

Each night a small complimentary chocolate was placed by each delegate's bed along with a glass of water, and the bed sheets were turned back. My delegates commented on this the following morning during our breakfast on the second day of the conference. One of our delegates commented to us that he had a coffee chocolate and he hates coffee so was disappointed. That night, without any prompting from any of us, alongside his bed sat two small chocolates, a glass of water and a small note from housekeeping saying simply this….. "I'm sorry about getting the chocolate wrong last night, please accept these two alternatives with my compliments…no coffee this time!"

We howled with laughter the following morning when he told us, but then thought, how did they know? The answer, one of the members of staff overheard the conversation at breakfast, and word got back to the housekeeping team, who noticed the coffee chocolate in the bin and corrected it the following evening. Now that's amazing and cultural – high level employee engagement embedded within the team so that surprising customers is the most normal thing in the world to them, and the staff loved doing it. The message constantly re-enforced by the leadership, the systems, the values, the training, the environment.

Imagine though, employing people in the hotel who didn't care about surprising the customer with this level of service, who didn't buy into *'surprise and delight'*. They would be quickly found out. The manager explained that they have sometimes recruited a person with the 'wrong' attitude, in that they didn't want to underpin the business values, and they were exposed very early in their 'probation' period. If they didn't respond to coaching and support, the rest of the staff simply wouldn't tolerate it.

Your task:
Review the tasks you have completed so far and make sure that all of the key elements align together to achieve your objectives, your vision and your values.

Take the time to identify the values of your employees using the questioning template described earlier. Remember that around 80% of a person's motivation will be linked to their top 4 or 5 values for the context in which you're asking. The majority of a person's work motivation is linked to their values for work. You should repeat this process typically every 6 months or so, since values will change over time.

Once you have identified a person's values, look for ways to link their values to your objectives. So if for example one of a person's values was 'learning', when you give them a new objective highlight, they will learn new things in meeting their objective. When the objective is complete, discuss the lessons learned and how they can be used in the future. Since we will typically identify 4 or 5 values, it should be relatively easy to link at least one value to the objective or task you are setting, and therefore gain the benefit of their natural motivation.

Consider the steps you can put in place to ensure that the business vision, values and objectives are communicated regularly and fully understood. I would suggest that you use visual communication for this as part of your overall strategy. People need constant reminders, so the vision and values need to be visible in the workplace, on screens, on walls and on whiteboards.

You might like to also consider how to give your employees the information and tools to make living the values easy to do. The conference venue in the example made sure that each employee had what they needed to easily demonstrate 'surprise and delight'. If you leave it to the employee to remember to do this, the majority certainly won't and you then have inconsistency and a diluted message. Make reminders systemic to make behaviour consistent.

Take every opportunity to remind people of how they are achieving your values and making progress towards your objectives. This is very easy to do by simply noticing and praising a person when they do something in line with your vision and values.

Identify ways to check progress of the alignment and engagement of the team. Ensure that people can air their concerns and celebrate success. There are some very effective employee engagement and feedback platforms available now. The important part is that employees will need the facility to communicate their concerns anonymously and be able to enter dialogue with senior leaders who can do something about the concerns raised. I would suggest that the alignment feedback process should be formally run every 3-6 months or so. The culture in a business can change fast, as Tom found out to his cost, and an annual survey just isn't frequent enough to keep the engagement process going.

Chapter 7 – Keeping the engagement going

Three months later…

Tom sat in the open park again, looking out over the countryside and out towards the sea. It was a lovely evening, peaceful, and he was taking the opportunity to reflect on the last few months. "Well you seem more relaxed than last time we met!" A startled Tom wheeled round to see the Magician strolling across the lawn towards him.

"Yes," said Tom "I am."

"Though I sense you have a question, something that's not quite clear in your mind?" added the Magician. His always welcome friend and mentor sat next to him on the bench.

"Hmm, yes" said Tom drawing out his answer and indicating that yet again The Magician had read his mind.

"You see, I'm really pleased with the way things have developed over the last few months. I'm sensing much greater buy-in from the team and better collaboration. They are solving problems quickly on their own. Andrea has done a fantastic job of implementing the revised vision of the business. Suja and Simon have put great sales systems in place and we are starting to see the fruits of their work with more business and the sales pipeline filling nicely.

It's interesting that people are more focussed and are taking the initiative again and that's showing in our customer delight feedback, and more referral business than we've ever had. It feels like we've got the leadership right, the systems right and everything is working well…"

"But something's bugging you?" added The Magician.

"Yes" reflected Tom. "I know we've identified the Rebels and pretty much got rid of most of the rebellious behaviour but I don't feel like we've finished."

"No you haven't - you never do. Your Stars always have the potential to become Rebels if you stop leading and managing well. It doesn't self perpetuate without any involvement from you. You need to keep looking for ways to keep your Stars as Stars, your Willing Helpers more like Stars, your Fence Sitters more like Willing Helpers, and maintain an environment that isn't attractive to Rebels. You've got the foundation, but the company keeps moving on."

"So where do the Stars go then? Surely they don't have to move on?"

"No, Tom, the Stars become magical leaders! Your challenge is not only developing the team, but also developing yourself, Andrea, and others in time, to be magical leaders, transforming and developing with the business over the long-term. These magical leaders would need to coach, would need to support, would need to mentor, so that the business develops and the people develop within it." He paused for effect. "Now, that's true leadership Tom, that's getting people to see and activate potential within themselves that they don't yet understand or recognise."

"How do you mean?" asked Tom.

"Well, Tom, would you agree that everyone has potential to be better at what they do, in any walk of life?"

"Within limits, yes!" said Tom. "It's not always easy to draw that potential out of a person, because sometimes they don't believe it's possible, or maybe it's too difficult."

"Exactly" exclaimed The Magician. "You, as a magical leader, spot the potential within the individual, often before they spot it in themselves, and through help and encouragement you draw out that ability until a person 'catches' themselves doing a task or acting in a way that they didn't think was possible. Then you make sure you praise them for it."

"To really engage your employees for the long-term, you will need to develop their abilities on an ongoing basis, so that you can give them more responsibility, almost without having to manage them. Overall there will be more Star and Willing Helper type behaviour than any other. Remember what we said about Willing Helpers, often just needing more confidence to become more like Stars. Stars just need to be trusted to get on with things, Fence Sitters want a vision to follow, and Rebels, often they need to be trusted enough to expose their bad habits so you can deal with them or have them flip into a Star and shine."

Tom nodded in acceptance, like The Magician had just confirmed a truth that Tom already knew. "Ok, so how do I keep it going then, how do I keep it fresh?"

"Ah right" said The Magician, "I thought we'd got to this point, excellent. As you can imagine, you will need to keep the structural elements we have already discussed in place to make sure you have the right culture or environment for people to thrive and engage."

The Magician handed Tom a small note with some reminders in place and started to re-cap each in turn.

Recall the structural elements to create the right culture:

★ *Setting the destination – clarity of vision and values.*

★ *The leadership message – consistently banging the drum, reminding the team what's important and why.*

★ *Systems and Processes – having working procedures for people to follow, systems of communication, systems of reward or penalty.*

★ *Capability – developing the skills and knowledge of the team, making sure that they are always on top of their game.*

★ *Behaviour – observing and noticing behaviours, both positive and negative, praising and reinforcing positive behaviours and correcting negatives ones.*

"OK" said Tom, "I've got that, a useful reminder for me to keep checking on the structural stuff. What else can I do to keep it going? I'm sure it won't just continue, I found that out with Andrea!"

The Magician smiled; "Exactly. The challenge we also have is that situations and people change. You can think that you're on top of things but how do you know? You have a business to run, customers to keep happy and new employees to hire. Let's face it, you very nearly lost your right-hand person and you didn't see it coming. If people begin to disengage, they probably won't tell you, and you might not be lucky and have a CV given to you next time."

Tom grimaced. He didn't really need reminding of this fact, or so he thought, but The Magician knew otherwise. Tom was about to begin taking his eye off the ball as he had in the past, and without some way of identifying potential Rebels and future Stars he could so easily fall into that trap again.

"What you need to do Tom is have a mechanism for gauging the level of engagement of the team, what's working, what isn't, people's opinions of you and your leadership team and how they feel about customer service, and whether they are being personally developed enough."

"That sounds like a lot of work for someone who unfortunately we don't have yet!" exclaimed Tom. "I'm guessing you're thinking about some kind of survey of staff and customers. The new HR and Development Manager can take care of that when he joins us hopefully in a month's time. I'm pleased that we stuck with the selection process we started – I think we've finally found the right person for our business. He said that he had experience of using some kind of platform to assess employee engagement as an ongoing thing."

"Well, it needn't be complicated," said The Magician. "There are plenty of very useful online portals which can do this for you now. The important thing is that whatever you do needs to offer anonymity for the commenter so they feel safe raising issues. You need a means of people communicating about concerns or ideas while still retaining that anonymity so that you can resolve issues before a person starts moving towards rebellion."

"The second part Tom are some activities which you and your leadership team need to do regularly from now on. These are behaviours which you will need to build into every working week."

"You mentioned Tom, that Andrea has implemented a revised vision and values for the business. How do you plan to re-connect the team with that on a regular basis?"

"I hadn't really thought about that," said Tom. "Once we've communicated it and everyone is familiar with it then surely they'll remember it?"

"Do you know your vision and values accurately from memory?" asked The Magician.

"Pretty much, but I take your point, not everyone will know or remember what's important unless we keep reminding them, so what do you suggest; that we have vision and values reminder sessions?"

"No Tom, like I said these things can be simple. What

about if you had visual signs around the workplace reminding people of your vision and values? As people demonstrate behaviour which is aligned with your values you can thank them and point at the signs to reinforce the message for them and others Equally if someone does something which is misaligned you can use the signs as a gentle reminder."

"Good idea" said Tom, "it's simple and would be a really useful reminder for everyone to stay on track."

"Right, second thing," said The Magician with a twinkle in his eye. "I know you've set goals with the teams and that Andrea creates performance statistics for the operations side of the business so you can discuss them in your management meetings. How do you share this information with the rest of the business, so that they can see the progress you're making and that they are part of a success story?"

Tom felt like he was being cornered, but he knew where The Magician was going with the conversation. Andrea had suggested that they should share some of the business results with the staff ages ago, but to Tom it seemed like a lot of work. He'd finally agreed to a simple update meeting for everyone quarterly, which they'd started yet in practice it hadn't been kept up. He tried to explain this rather feebly to The Magician, who just sat there and smiled as Tom looked very uncomfortable.

The Magician pointed out at the sailing yachts in the distance. "Let me ask you Tom, if you were part of a crew tasked with racing a yacht from point A to point B within a certain time, but the skipper kept refusing to give you basic information like speed, distance covered, wind direction and strength, or about your progress against the competition, how would you feel? Frustrated? Disengaged maybe?"

Tom sighed, "I take your point, so what sort of information should we be sharing?"

"You know your business Tom, so you would be a good judge of that, but I'd start with the information which Andrea shares at the management meeting. If you think about the information you provide being broadly under the headings of quality, cost, delivery, people, and safety you'd be along the right lines."

Let's start with quality, what information do you need Tom to know that the quality you give your customers is right?"

"Well, I'd like some customer feedback, but how do I measure that?" replied Tom. "There are a number of ways," said The Magician. "For example you could ask your customers to give you a score for the different parts of their experience, and then show all the scores as an average from those customers who responded.

"Do you give customers a promised delivery date?" quizzed The Magician.

"Yes of course!" exclaimed Tom. "In fact that's one of Andrea's great prides, she loves to tell us in the management meeting that everything she agreed with clients happens on time!"

"Do you tell the rest of the people involved in the business about such great success to generate pride within them?" The Magician asked, looking sideways at

Tom, already knowing the answer but asking it cheekily anyway.

"Ah" said Tom, "I take your point. I guess that's our delivery measure to be put on the whiteboard you suggested then?"

"Absolutely," smiled The Magician. "So we have examples for quality and delivery, what about cost, do you estimate how long it takes to do a job?"

"Yes of course" said Tom, "how could we price it for the client without doing that?"

"I see," smiled The Magician. "And you have timesheets for the actual time taken?"

"I see where you're going with this," chipped in Tom. "If we compared estimated time to the actual time taken we can show if our costs are under control."

"Correct," said The Magician. "You're really getting this Tom, well done." The sarcasm from The Magician surprised Tom, it wasn't like him to speak that way, Tom was visibly taken aback. The Magician smiled warmly at Tom. "I'm sorry," said The Magician, "I couldn't resist it. There's a fine line between being supportive and patronising when bringing this information to the team, and I wanted you to know the difference."

"Point taken," said Tom. "I've got to be careful how we communicate this to the team so it seems relevant and interesting."

"What I suggest Tom is that you need to share the information visually, exactly as you say, you need to agree with Andrea what information is relevant to who, and then how frequently you share it, probably monthly.

I think you'll find that quarterly is too far apart and weekly might be difficult to collate. You have a start now anyway."

"Next thing, standards!" declared The Magician, looking seriously at Tom. "How did Rory get to the point where he was taking extra time for lunch, along with his buddies by the way, and nothing was said to him despite it causing some frustration for many people?"

Tom opened his mouth to respond and closed it again, thinking better of even attempting a defence. He had none, and he knew it. "This is a critical piece of keeping things going," said The Magician. "Your employees are expecting you to uphold standards. You know we discussed earlier putting the values on signs on the wall, they will only *remind* people of standards but they won't *manage* them for you Tom, that's your job as a leader, praise behaviour you want, but also tackle behaviour you don't."

Having made his point The Magician switched state in an instant to lighten the mood. "How's young Chris getting on?" he asked brightly. "He's doing rather well actually," said Tom. "He seems to have really engaged with his new role dealing with the customers for Rory. I think he's thriving on the extra responsibility."

"Excellent," said The Magician, "that's another key element of keeping this going, always look for opportunities for people to take extra responsibility, as we discussed earlier,. It helps them grow and they feel like they're making progress and being trusted which will increase their levels of engagement. The extra responsibility doesn't have to be much, and you certainly don't want to overload people, otherwise you might generate Rebel behaviour, but knowing each person's limits and their work values will help you make some good choices."

"Be sure to look for and act upon opportunities to praise people for their work though Tom, that's vitally important."

"Right then, last but by no means least, teamwork. When was the last time you pulled the team together to get their ideas about how to improve things, or perhaps celebrated success with a team building day?" The Magician looked squarely at Tom and was silent.

"Too long," sighed Tom. "I know it's too long but I've been too busy to organise anything, you know that."

"What about asking your employees - led by your Stars and Willing Helpers - to organise it for themselves. Why not give them a budget and some parameters and let them get on with it. What's the matter Tom, don't you trust them?" jibed The Magician.

Tom knew The Magician had a point. Why didn't he let them get on with it, they were capable people, happy to take on additional responsibility. No, the fault was with Tom for not letting go. Finally, Tom returned the stare of his companion. "You have a way of making me face my challenges my friend. I will change, if I want my employees to engage fully I need to allow them to do so, you have my word.".

The Magician smiled broadly. "Excellent," he said, "excellent, well here's your reminder Tom. Let me know when you need me next."

The Magician handed Tom the second piece of paper of the evening, Tom quickly read its contents, knowing it would be a helpful reminder of this evening's conversation.

Clarity – Remind people regularly of the purpose of their role and the business, give them clarity of their objectives and how they individually are contributing towards the company purpose.

Commitment – Demonstrate your commitment to your objectives by communicating progress towards your goals, good and bad, to all key stakeholders, especially your team. Demonstrate commitment to achieving the goals set by training and developing them.

Standards – Be the best role model of the company standards of behaviour and action, and tackle any examples of people letting standards slip at any level. The rest of the team are watching what you do and following your lead.

Responsibility – Trust people to get on with things and don't interfere. Checking in with people to answer any questions or give encouragement is a *good idea. Checking on people and their progress will demoralise them.*

Recognition – Praise for a job well done, as often as is necessary for the individual – remember their values!

Teamwork – set team objectives and encourage the team to celebrate differences rather than arguing about them.

"The most important aspect of your role as a leader Tom, is to develop people so that they can take some of your responsibilities off you and your senior team. After all it's what you did with Andrea from the beginning, it's just that you didn't continue the process in developing more capacity across the senior team, which stifled the business and overburdened Andrea." The Magician waited for a moment to see if Tom reacted, and noted the reflective look on Tom's face. He then continued when he was sure he had Tom's full attention:

"You my friend, have got to become a facilitator of others' growth and development – a coach if you like, having meaningful and regular development conversations with the members of your team, so that they in turn do the same with their teams. You need to create a culture of constant development. The more you develop, the more trust you'll generate, the more ideas and suggestions you'll get for improvement through the communication and survey process we discussed earlier. People love to contribute and make progress, and you need to support that."

"I see" said Tom, "So actually we become a bit like you!" As Tom closed his eyes to reflect inwardly on his likely role in the future, he felt completely immersed in the idea and what it might entail. Enough time to discover that when he opened his eyes a few moments later The Magician was gone.

"A magical leader! A Magician creating magic in people and teams!" Tom murmured as he took one last look over the peaceful twilight fields and headed back across the lawn for home.

Concept 7
Key dimensions of employee engagement

There is much to review about employee engagement and how to maintain the momentum once you have your team and their approach on track. The key to making this work is to keep things simple. After all, if you are running a business or an organisation, it's not your objective to have engaged employees, your objective is to have a successful organisation achieving its aims. It just happens that if you have fully engaged teams; your customers, your employees, in fact all of your stakeholders, are likely to have a much better experience of interacting with your organisation, and you are more likely to achieve your, or your business' goals.

The steps outlined through this chapter and throughout the book will create a climate which supports growth, development and success. There are a few key dimensions which support ongoing employee engagement and these were outlined through Tom's conversation with The Magician. They are as follows:

Clarity
Make sure that your employees remain absolutely crystal clear about the purpose of the business and of the team they are in. They need clarity of their objectives and how they contribute towards the overall vision. They also need to know how their own objectives relate to everyone else in the chain.

If people understand the part they play in the future success of the organisation or team, they are much more likely to contribute towards that success.

Questions we can use to identify the team or business purpose are:
- What are we here for?
- What is the team purpose?
- How do we want to be described?
- What do we want to achieve?
- What do we contribute to the rest of the organisation?

These are all questions you will need to help them find answers to, so that they give of their best.

Every employee should have a clear line of sight between the purpose and objectives of the organisation, and the purpose and objectives of their job. When people feel that they are contributing to a purpose that they understand and support, then they are likely to be more motivated. We can then tap into that motivation for the good of the individual and the organisation.

One of the challenges we face with keeping people engaged is that they are easily distracted. We are inquisitive beings, something new and interesting can draw our attention from 'the familiar stuff' which will probably be ignored for the time being. So, the next task is to keep the purpose alive and front of mind through regular communication.

Communicating commitment

We have to gain and demonstrate ongoing commitment to the vision or purpose. The problem is that once it's familiar and we understand it, there's nothing new to it, so it is at risk of becoming part of the background. To keep the purpose alive, we need to keep referring to our mission, vision and values in new and different ways. Some of these are obvious, some not so.

The first and most obvious, is that you should have visual examples of the mission, vision, and values, all around the organisation; on the walls in words, in pictures, on mugs, on computer desk tops - don't be afraid of over communicating it. You need reference points everywhere, especially where people meet and talk. It's all part of the subliminal message of the organisation.

The next stage is to keep linking to these visual examples. So when you see some activity which demonstrates connection to the purpose, take the opportunity to highlight the good work and refer to the appropriate visual reminder. Equally, if you see behaviour which is at odds with the purpose, take the opportunity to point to the reminder and highlight what could be done differently to better support the purpose. For example you might have awards for employees who best embody each value.

Finally, report progress towards the organisation objectives, in the form of goals achieved or results compared to the KPIs agreed with the team. It is important that such information is visible to all, and that the performance or results are explained regularly. This shows that you are prepared to communicate the results, good or bad, so that the team understand progress that has been made and any necessary changes to drive further progress.

Remember that you need to show a connection between your Vision and Values and the objectives or KPIs. The best way to do this is to link each KPI to the appropriate value. For example, if one of the company values is 'reliability', a measure to identify reliability might be 'on-time delivery' and you can show as a score the percentage of your orders which were completed on time in full – therefore communicating progress towards your KPIs and so your values.

A simple visual management system might have the values listed, within each value a series of KPIs which link to those values and a KPI target, then alongside the target the actual performance. If the actual performance falls short of the target, there should be an explanation and actions listed which are intended to push the performance to meet the target KPI during the next period, probably monthly

An example table can be seen below:

Value	Objective	Units	Target	Actual	√ /X	Issues/ Reason
Quality	Customer satisfaction score	/10	9	8	x	Excess corrective actions at end of project
Delivery	Orders completed on time	%	100	100	√	
Cost	Project spend on budget	%	95	98	√	
Value	Action	By who		By When		Measure of completion
Quality	Review corrective actions list and identify how they can be avoided on future projects					

Consistency of standards

Good leaders will naturally encourage people to work to and demonstrate high standards, it's a natural expectation. Maintaining high standards of quality, performance, and discipline sets the tone for the way the team are meant to work now and in the future. If you, as a leader, allow your standards to slip, you are potentially signalling a future fall in the performance of the team. I remember working with a manager who had very high standards in the way he interacted with his team, the way he shared information, the quality of his reports, and he carried utmost respect from everyone he worked with.

Interestingly, his team followed his lead in the quality of work and the respectful nature of communication within the team and with him.

Confidence and responsibility

Logically, once you have set the standard you want in terms of the organisation's values and reminded people of those standards at every opportunity, it's important that you let the team get on with achieving the objectives which you have set. Clearly your management style will depend on the behaviour of the individuals being led – you will manage a Star slightly differently than a Willing Helper. Nonetheless, it is important that people are allowed to take responsibility for their objectives. It shows them that you trust them and the level of support you provide should give them confidence in their ability to complete the task.

The worst possible thing to do with an employee is to micromanage their performance. If you do, in effect your actions are saying "I don't trust you – you're incapable" and are likely to generate resentment and frustration from all concerned. By all means review progress with objectives, and reiterate why the objectives set are important, maybe providing guidance and support if they need it, but the individual should be allowed to determine how they plan to tackle the task so that they can take the credit for the task when it is completed. This takes us neatly on to...

Recognition

Consider this question just for a moment: How does a person know they have done a good job? It's an interesting question when you start to think about it. You'd also think that the answer is obvious – when they see the completed job. But how do they know they've done a GOOD job, to the right standard? It is a rare individual who uses only self-reference to confirm a good job. The rest of us will need some form of feedback, from a customer, a colleague or a boss.

Yet I hear all too often managers asking "why do my employees need constant praise, surely they know when they've done a good job?" The answer is of course, no they don't, unless someone tells them. Remember, individuals who self-reference, usually have lots of confidence and are either already a Star or in a leadership role. If you want consistently good performance, you have to give consistently fair and balanced feedback. Recognise good work, and if appropriate make a suggestion or request for possible improvement.

A colleague introduced me to a simple framework which I have used and as it works really well, so I will explain it here

There are five simple stages and the process can be used to give both positive and corrective feedback:

1. Describe the **event** behaviour or result you observed – what did you see?
2. Explain the **effect** or outcome of the behaviour / result you observed.
3. Describe your **reaction** or that of others to the result.
4. Explain that you **recognise** the challenges or circumstances surrounding the event.
5. **Request** what you want the person to do now.

Example - positive feedback:

1. I observed you serving that customer well (**event**).
2. The customer was very happy and you were a role model for others to follow (**effect**).
3. I felt very proud of your performance (**reaction**).
4. I recognise you have worked hard at getting that right (**recognise**).
5. Keep up the good work (**request**).

Example - corrective feedback:

1. I observed you getting impatient with your colleague (**event**).

2. The more impatient you got, it caused your communication to fail (**effect**).

3. It was frustrating for your colleague and embarrassing for us in the meeting (**reaction**).

4. I recognise you feel passionate about this subject (**recognise**).

5. Next time give people their chance to express an idea, so you understand their perspective (**request**).

There are many ways to recognise good performance in the form of bonuses and prizes, and celebrations, and they all work at the appropriate time, but there is absolutely no replacement for sincerely delivered praise and feedback. Good leaders generate great loyalty by using this practice well.

Teamwork

The final sustaining dimension which maintains and builds upon creating the right culture, is Teamwork. If you want good performance to be sustainable, there is nothing quite like the power of a team. A team will apply peer pressure to maintain standards far more effectively than a manager could, and the team take great pride in supporting each other. Fostering teamwork is an absolute must in sustaining high levels of employee engagement. The interesting thing is that it is often so simple to create in the first place, in that it's really about setting goals for the team, to be achieved by the team.

We can make teamwork more complex by identifying the different personalities of team members and how they can complement each-others' traits in order to get the best from the overall team.

Suffice to say that if you pay attention as a team manager, you will notice each team member's relative strengths and weaknesses, how the team interact, who are the ones who like to take the lead, who like to finish things off, the ideas people, the ones who like things to be practical and down to earth, and the ones who are good at keeping people happy.

To notice all this you will of course need to set and agree some objectives for the team, which can only be achieved as a team for these full dynamics to show themselves. As we covered in the section of Confidence and Responsibility, once you have set the team goal, it's important that you let the team get on with it, create the plan, and go for the goal. It's your job to cheer them on from the side lines, giving feedback as highlighted above.

Your task:
Consider what you can do as a leader to reinforce the values, ethos, and atmosphere you want with your team.

How can you reinforce the direction/purpose of the team?

What ways can you use to communicate progress or revisit your most important goals?

Who else in your team can help you lead and how do you enlist their help?

Identify ways to keep your vision and values fresh and alive using the hints from the list The Magician gave to Tom.

Summary / conclusion

Throughout the story of Tom, his encounter with Stars and Rebels and his help from The Magician, the behaviour of different team members was examined, causes of that behaviour were uncovered and the way behaviour can change over time was explored.

If you reflect on your own experiences, you will probably be able to think of times when you have behaved as a Star or a Willing Helper. There are probably other times when you have been a Fence Sitter or a Rebel. As you think of occasions when you have strongly exhibited each of those behaviours, consider the factors that contributed to the way you behaved.

Was leadership behaviour an influence? Were you being led by someone you admired, being clear and consistent in what they wanted, and who included you and made you feel valued?

How did the systems and procedures support you? Did the systems and procedures fit with what the leader wanted; so that you knew what the priorities were for your work and any potential for conflicting priorities were minimised?

How were your capabilities used? Was there a good match between the skills and experience you had and what you were being asked to do? Given your ability were you provided with the right support, and was this the same for the rest of the team?

When these things are all aligned then the behaviours you see are positive. Whenever negative behaviours show it is a sign or symptom of something wrong at a deeper level. Learning to view behaviour in the simple terms of Stars, Willing Helpers, Fence Sitters, and Rebels, will help you a great deal in your role as a leader. But remember, the challenge is that your organisation and team are constantly changing. You can't stop change, all you can do is respond to it. As a leader, your role is to constantly work to keep your organisation and team in balance, no matter what changes come along.

Tom's been on a journey. He made some mistakes. With The Magician beside him he's learned a huge amount and the journey never ends. He can see himself as a Star Leader. That's the excitement of working with teams and the thrill of seeing them flourish.

So, what about you, are you up for it? Then make a start.

Author's note

Creating 'Tom the sequel' has been at the back of my mind for a long time. We have been using the first book as a training resource for many years, and the feedback has consistently been that people relate to Tom and the decisions he's making. A very common comment when we discuss the book with delegates is 'it's like reading about myself'. It would seem that using the format of a story combined with reflections on the key concepts has proven to be very effective. After all, some of the most enduring lessons of life have been told through stories and metaphors.

As with so many lessons in life, we learn from experience, even if it is through the experience of others. Arguably that is the best experience to learn from. Reading about Tom and The Magician allows you to do just that.

The lessons covered in this book could be applied to almost any walk of life. Whether you are in business, the public sector or working with a charity or a church, you will no doubt face the same challenges as Tom, and you will have to find solutions to them. Similarly Tom could be another gender from any background, and the family represent any family unit that may apply to you.

Employee Engagement & Leadership

Over the last 2 decades I have trained large numbers of people in the art of leadership, and during that time I have often heard people say, 'But I haven't got time to step-back and look at these issues.' My response is always 'As long as you don't make time for it, you won't have time'.

Eventually, circumstances will make you sit up and pay attention, in whatever form that takes – staff turnover, discomfort, illness, absenteeism, conflict with others to name but a few. The symptoms are many and varied, and all too often they are well known. Please heed the signal. If you ignore it, the signal will just take louder and more extreme forms until you do take notice.

The issues which Tom has to face at the beginning of the story are his 'wake-up call', and they are largely of his own making. What Tom discovers is that the seeds for his troubles were set some time ago.

What Tom discovers with the help of The Magician, is that if you have aligned and engaged people in your team, you will find it much easier to generate great results. If you engender trust within the team you will find it easier to access a person's inner motivation to serve you and your customers well, and create a great experience for everyone involved.

As within the first book it's all down to how Tom leads and inspires, to generate amazing results from ordinary people.

So now it's over to you.

Bibliography

There are many books which will have contributed to this one, sometimes it's just an idea which another source builds upon. Here are a few of the ones, that really stick in my mind.

Good to Great by Jim Collins ISBN 978-0-712676-09-0

Built to Last by Jim Collins ISBN 1-8441-3584-5

The 7 Habits of Highly Effective People
by Stephen R. Covey ISBN 978-0-684858-39-5

The 8th Habit: From Effectiveness to Greatness
by Stephen R. Covey ISBN 978-0-743206-83-9

The Virgin Way
by Richard Branson ISBN 978-0-753519-88-2

Realigning for Change: 8 Principles for Successful Change Management in Your Organisation by David Molden & Jon. Symes ISBN 978-0-273633-81-5

Maverick! by Ricardo Semler ISBN 978-0-712678-86-5

Onward by Howard Schultz ISBN 978-1-119-977-23-0

About the Author

Charles Barnascone is the founder and Managing Director of Infinite Possibilities Ltd, a company dedicated to helping businesses grow by developing their leadership, and their ability to generate more sales.

Charles is a highly experienced trainer, coach and business development consultant. He has managed Infinite Possibilities Ltd for the last 23 years and during this time has worked with a large number of diverse businesses across the UK.

His career in sales and management has spanned 36 years and this has afforded him a huge variety of experiences both personally and through others. He uses these within his training, adding a great deal of realism with energy and flair.

Charles has expertise in dealing with decision makers at a very senior level in organisations of all sizes, and he is very passionate about the necessity for leaders to truly engage people personally.

He has researched, written and delivered many training programmes dealing with management, sales, team building, personal effectiveness, and leadership, and created the Leadership Matrix™ detailed within his first book.